Japan's Economic Performance
and International Role

Japan's Economic Performance and International Role

Yoshio Suzuki

UNIVERSITY OF TOKYO PRESS

Publication of this volume was supported
by a grant from The Japan Foundation.

Printed in Japan
ISBN 4-13-047043-4 (Japan)
ISBN 0-86008-445-0

Contents

Preface vii

Part I   Inside the Japanese Economy

1   Price Stability and Stable Growth under
    the Floating Exchange Rate System 5
2   The High-Yen Recession and Revival of
    Stable Growth since 1985 39

Part II   Japan's Role in the World Economy

3   Can a World Depression Recur? 93
4   Japan's Role in the Future Monetary
    System 111
5   The Steady Course of Financial Reform 137

Index 173

Preface

Sixteen years have passed since the end of the 18-year rapid economic growth period, the so-called Japanese miracle, during which Japan's economy recorded an average annual growth rate of 10 percent.

The end of high-speed growth coincided with the breakdown of the Bretton Woods system, which for nearly three postwar decades combined a gold standard with the U.S. dollar as the key currency and an adjustable peg. It also coincided with the advent of the first oil crisis. Under the subsequently adopted floating exchange rate system, Japan's economy has experienced further shocks of external origin, including a second oil crisis, substantial appreciation in the value of the dollar, and its subsequent even more remarkable fall.

The performance of the Japanese economy and the ways in which it has managed to overcome such external shocks in the past 16 years, although not as widely discussed as rapid growth, have been remarkable. While Japan achieved the highest average growth rate among major industrial countries for this period, the recent inflation rate, as meas-

ured by the rise in consumer prices, has been the lowest—
even lower than in the Federal Republic of Germany. The
nominal exchange value of the yen has undergone the greatest appreciation among the leading currencies.

I have participated in many international conferences
and meetings during the past several years, as Director of
the Bank of Japan's Institute for Monetary and Economic
Studies and, since early 1988, as an Executive Director of
the Bank in charge of economic research. Such meetings
include the annual Monetary Experts Meeting of the OECD;
conferences organized by the U.S. Federal Reserve Board,
regional Federal Reserve banks, and European central banks;
and various privately sponsored meetings. These international
forums have provided me with opportunities to explain the
background to Japan's economic performance and to present
my view on its role in the world economy.

The more meetings I attend, the more strongly I feel that
while discussion with other specialists is extremely useful,
it is not sufficient. I have become more and more convinced
that there is a need for Japanese economists to explain to
a wider audience the basic trends in Japan's economy, to
give their views about Japan's role in the world, and to
seek critical and constructive comments on that role.

This volume is an attempt to undertake at least part of
this formidable task. It is based on papers which I prepared
for various meetings and on a book written in Japanese
(*Sekai no naka no Nihon keizai to kinyū* [*Japan's Economy and
Monetary System in a World Context*]), from which several chapters have been translated. The current text has undergone
several revisions and additions both for the purpose of up-
dating and also for facilitating understanding by nonspecialist
readers.

The book consists of two parts. Part I, "Inside the
Japanese Economy," deals with basic trends in Japan's
economy. In Chapter 1, economic performance during

the 16 years since the end of the rapid-growth period is discussed; this chapter examines how stable, relatively high growth was reconciled with low inflation in comparison with other major industrial countries. Chapter 2 is devoted to the causes of the rapid and substantial appreciation of the yen after the Plaza Accord of September 1985, the deflationary impact on the Japanese economy of the yen's recent appreciation, and the revival of stable growth.

As the title "Japan's Role in the World Economy" reveals, Part II is more normative. Chapter 3 compares the present situation with the great depression of 1929–1933 and discusses the role Japan as the largest creditor country should play in ensuring the stability and growth of the world economy. Chapter 4 discusses the future of the international monetary system and considers the role the yen and Japan's money and capital markets should play in that system. The advantages and disadvantages of the flexible exchange rate system, competition and cooperation among multiple currencies and financial centers, and the progress of horizontal trade between Asian countries are topics given particular emphasis. In Chapter 5 I present my view regarding the direction financial reform should take in order for Japan to fulfill its role in the future international monetary system.

Although the focus is on the Japanese economy, I have also referred to experiences in other major industrial economies and their financial markets, indicating similarities and differences. I will be gratified if this book succeeds in helping readers outside Japan to better understand the Japanese economy and in eliciting constructive comments from overseas on Japan's future role.

I am deeply indebted to all the economists in central banks and academic circles who offered me the opportunity to participate in various meetings and who have made useful comments. It would not have been possible to publish this book in its present form without the personal contribution of IMF economist Dr. Robert Feldman in translating the previously published Japanese portions of the text into English, and the support of the Forum for Policy Innovation. Last but not least, the efforts of the staff of the University of Tokyo Press were indispensable for the timely publication of this volume. This book is truly a joint effort.

Part I

Inside the Japanese Economy

Part I of this book discusses developments in the macro-economic performance of Japan during the period from the shift to a floating exchange rate up to 1988. Included are discussions of the how and why of economic growth, inflation, balance of payments, and exchange rates. Developments in the major industrial countries are also touched on, although Japan will be the main focus of attention. Still, in considering what occurred in Japan, one must also consider the international environment in which the Japanese economy operates. It is obviously necessary to discuss Japan's relations with foreign economies and their differences and similarities.

Chapter 1 details the main features of the macroeconomic performance of Japan under the floating exchange rate system as compared with that under the pre-1973 fixed exchange rate system and with that of other industrialized countries under the same system. Chapter 2 focuses on developments in the Japanese economy since the Plaza Accord of September 1985: how it was affected by the tremendous appreciation of the yen and how it attained a stable pattern of domestic demand-led growth.

3

1

Price Stability and Stable Growth
under the Floating Exchange Rate System

One main feature of macroeconomic performance in Japan since the shift to floating exchange rates has been the reduction in the variability of inflation and growth. In this sense, one may say that macroeconomic performance in Japan has stabilized under the floating exchange rate system. Other main features have been the emergence of a large current account surplus in the 1980s and Japan's becoming the world's major creditor nation.

Low Inflation and High Growth

The reduction in variability of inflation and growth and the stabilization of macroeconomic performance are outlined in Figure 1. This figure shows the growth rate of money stock together with that of nominal and real GNP over the years 1956 to 1988 in terms of quarterly data vis-à-vis the same quarter of the previous year. Because the Bank of Japan switched to a policy of focusing attention on M2 + CDs in 1975, this broader indicator of the money stock, which includes currency, demand deposits, time deposits, and certificates of deposit, is used in the figure. The following aspects of macro performance may be read from it.

In the period from 1956 to 1973, in which real growth was very high, the money stock experienced large fluctuations in growth rates. Because, under a fixed exchange rate system, a tight monetary policy had to be adopted during balance of payments crises, money growth fell to as low as 15 percent; but when balance of payments problems ended, a loose monetary policy allowed money growth to rise to as much as 25 percent. Nominal GNP growth largely followed the same pattern once the lags of several quarters are allowed for, suggesting that the causal relationship flowed from the money stock to nominal GNP. Moreover, these fluctuations in the growth rate of nominal GNP accompanied fluctuations in the growth rate of real GNP and inflation as seen in the GNP deflator. (The movements of inflation as seen in the GNP deflator are shown in the graph as the difference between the growth rate of nominal GNP and that of real GNP.) As a result, the discretionary changes in monetary policy in response to balance of payments brought about large changes in monetary growth and great instability in both the real growth rate and the inflation rate, even though they still attained an average high growth of about 10 percent along with average inflation of about 6 percent.

Let us next look at the macroeconomic performance of Japan since 1975, after the direct effects of the shift to floating exchange rates and the effects of the first oil crisis had worn off.

Gradual decline of monetary growth as a stabilization policy

Once the Bank of Japan began to focus attention on the money supply as an intermediate target, around 1975, the fluctuations in the growth rate of the money stock were reduced, and the deviations from the trend were limited to plus or minus 2.5 percent. Moreover, the trend of money growth itself fell during this period from about 15 percent at the start to 7–8 percent in 1983–1985—that is, until the Plaza Accord of September 1985. As a result, the nominal growth rate of GNP fell as well.

The fall in the growth rate of nominal GNP did not have any influence on the growth rate of real GNP, however, but rather was reflected in a decline in inflation as measured by the GNP deflator. This development is of great importance. With the two exceptions of the period around 1982 and that around 1986, growth over the entire period was very stable, averaging about 5 percent. The first period of exception was around the time of the second oil crisis when double-digit inflation required the major industrial countries to cooperate in taking concerted disinflationary policies and thus included the effect of adverse demand shocks from abroad in the form of the simultaneous world recession. The second period of exception was that of the substantial yen revaluation after the Plaza Accord of September 1985.

To summarize, Figure 1 suggests the following important points: The discretionary management of monetary policy in response to balance-of-payment changes that brought rapid changes in the growth rate of money in the period before 1974 had a strong effect on both real growth and inflation rates, and this was a factor in destabilizing the macroeconomy in Japan. However, events and experiences since 1975 suggest that lower inflation and a stabilization of macroeconomic performance—that is, of inflation rate and economic growth rate—can be achieved by stabilizing monetary growth rates and gradually allowing them to decline.

As a result, Japan's recent inflation rates in terms of consumer prices are the lowest and its real growth rates are still the highest among the five major industrialized countries. This is confirmed by the data in Table 1. Since the shift to the floating exchange rate system in 1973, Japan's inflation rates have been declining; in the 1982–1987 period the average inflation rate was 1.6%, the lowest among the five major industrialized countries, while Japan's average real growth rates from 1974 through 1987, including the two exceptional periods, averaged a bit less than 4%, which was still the highest among the five, although less than half that of the pre-1973 level.

Flexibility of real wages

How are we to interpret this attainment of stable inflation and economic growth rates? It may be hypothesized that there were two main factors that formed the background for it. First is the fact that the labor market in Japan is of a form very close to that suggested by the classical model of the labor market, in which real wages are sufficiently flexible always to equilibrate demand for and supply of labor. In such a situation, an economy grows on the stable path of equilibrium in which profit maximization of business firms is sustained. Second, monetary policy was managed in such a way that actual inflation rates did not deviate by large amounts or over a long period from the expectations held by agents in the labor market. According to standard economics textbooks, which are based on the natural rate of unemployment hypothesis, an economy of this type will have a vertical long-run Phillips curve so that with declining money growth, stable real growth may be maintained while the inflation rate is gradually lowered as the economy climbs down the Phillips curve.

To expand on this point, the major difference between classical and Keynesian economics is the stickiness of the nominal wage in the Keynesian. In the classical view, real wages are flexible. The Keynesian theory of the sticky nominal wage is based on the existence of long-term contracts

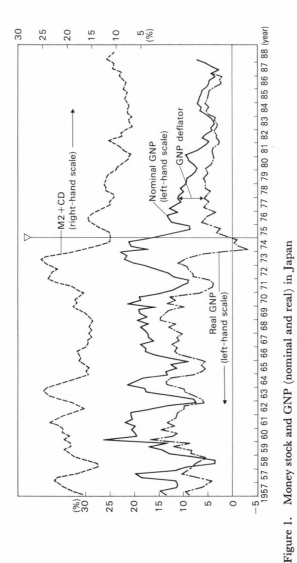

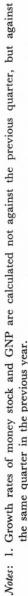

Figure 1.   Money stock and GNP (nominal and real) in Japan

Notes: 1. Growth rates of money stock and GNP are calculated not against the previous quarter, but against the same quarter in the previous year.

2. M2+CD data (before 1979/I, M2 data) are averages of end-of-month observations. For example, the first quarter is an average of the data for the end of January, February, and March.

Table 1. Economic growth rates and inflation rates after introduction of the floating exchange rate system.

	Real GNP* (% average annual growth rate)		Consumer price index (% average annual change rate)		
	1974–1979	1980–1987	1974–1977	1978–1981	1982–1987
Japan	3.6	3.9	13.0	5.1	1.6
United States	2.6	2.4	8.1	10.7	3.8
Federal Republic of Germany	2.3	1.5	5.2	4.6	2.2
France	3.3	1.7	11.1	11.7	6.7
United Kingdom	1.5	1.8	18.1	12.8	5.3

* For France and the United Kingdom, GDP is used.

and on such institutional factors as the high level of adjustment costs of wages. Such factors, however, seem to have only a tenuous relationship in Japan, and therefore it would seem that Japan is closer to the classical model than to the Keynesian one.

Some details may be of interest. First, basic wages in Japan in most cases are determined year by year in an annual spring labor negotiations offensive. It is uncommon for wage contracts to be of more than two years' duration. Moreover, bonuses and overtime payments comprise between one quarter and one fifth of total annual income in Japan, and this portion of income is much more flexible than the basic wage. Amounts paid in bonuses traditionally reflect the short-term profit performance of enterprises and fluctuate very flexibly between the semiannual payments. Overtime payments are of course related to overtime work hours and therefore reflect the level of activity in a firm. These are therefore highly flexible as well. In summary, wage adjustment costs during the year are not high. Moreover, the wage settlements in the spring offensive have been shown by many empirical studies to reflect not only past and expected inflation but also the demand-supply balance in the labor markets and the state of corporate profits. The results of the spring offensive are therefore quite sensitive to economic factors. Because of this flexibility in real wages, it is realistic to hypothesize that firms are almost continuously in a state of equilibrium.

Another reason why it is easy for Japanese firms to achieve states of equilibrium is that the growth rates of labor productivity in Japan are high. Equilibrating the marginal productivity of labor with adjustments in real wages is a necessary condition for profit maximizing of firms and brings about the equilibrium of the firms. Not only are real wages more flexible in Japan; the marginal productivity of labor has also grown faster than in other industrialized

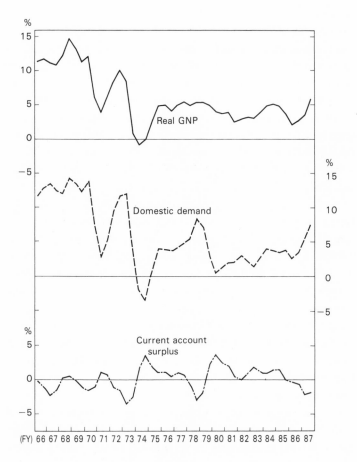

Figure 2. Growth rate of real GNP and contribution of the two components of aggregate demand, as year-to-year changes.

Note: Both domestic demand and current account surplus are adjusted to exclude effects of the import of gold bullion to mint coins in commemoration of the Emperor's 60-year reign.

countries. This has been a factor in the ability of Japanese firms to recover equilibrium easily.

Self-sustained economic growth

In the classical model, the supply side of the economy sets the economic growth path because the labor market is always in an equilibrium, and thus the supply capacity in equilibrium always determines growth. On the contrary, in the Keynesian model, the demand side establishes the growth path because the labor market is usually in disequilibrium, the supply capacity is not fully used, and thus the aggregate demand controlled by macroeconomic policies always determines the growth path.

In reality, since 1975, which side of the Japanese economy has mainly determined that stable growth path? Figure 2 suggests the answer. In this chart, it is confirmed again that the growth path since 1975 has been stable at about an annual 5% growth rate except for the two periods around 1982 and 1986. Surprisingly, however, the two components of aggregate demand, domestic demand and current account surplus, have not been stable at all since 1975. They have instead fluctuated as widely as during the pre-1975 period when the growth rate was quite unstable. Therefore, the factor responsible for the difference in the stability of economic growth between the pre- and post-1975 periods does not appear to be on the demand side. The main responsibility seems attributable to the fact that the Japanese economy had often deviated from equilibrium before 1975, but has been in equilibrium since 1975, with two exceptional periods. An economy in equilibrium always follows a stable growth path in line with stable growth of the supply capacity. In such an economy, fluctuation of one component of aggregate demand is canceled out by fluctuations of the other component through real crowding-out effects, since total aggregate demand is always constrained by the stable supply capacity of the economy. This was the case for the self-sustained, stable growth of the Japanese economy from 1975 to 1988.

Features of monetary targeting

Why, then, has the Japanese economy since 1975 not deviated much from equilibrium? One plausible interpretation is that Japanese monetary policy after 1975 did not permit major deviations of actual from expected inflation, so that the economy did not deviate from a vertical long-run Phillips curve.

The monetary targeting implemented by the Bank of Japan since 1975 has three major features. First, a broad definition of money (M2 + CDs) has been the most important intermediate target. Second, the term measured is not a week, a month, or even a quarter, but an entire year, so that the growth rate of money compared with the same period in the previous year is used. Third, actual targets are not publicized; rather, forecast values are announced that refer to the average money stock outstanding relative to the same period in the previous year for each quarter.

The rationale for Japan using M2 + CDs is also of interest. Although the contemporaneous correlation between nominal expenditure and M1 is larger in Japan than that between nominal expenditure and M2 + CDs, there is an even higher correlation between nominal expenditure in a current quarter and M2 + CDs growth in the prior four to six quarters. Moreover, for M1 and income, contemporaneous correlation also shows some causality running from income and expenditure to M1, and therefore the central bank cannot fully control current period expenditure or income through the control of M1. What is important for the control by a central bank of the money supply is a monetary indicator that has a close relationship with the income and expenditure that will be realized in the future. Because M2+CDs has a stronger relationship with future expenditure and income than does M1, the former was chosen as the intermediate target.

The timing of effects is also of interest. The value of M2+CDs in a current quarter exerts influence on nominal expenditure in the subsequent eight quarters. To put this another way, the money supply in any given quarter has only a small influence on the nominal income in any particular quarter in the future. This implies that strict control of the money supply over one month or over one quarter is not very meaningful from the viewpoint of stabilizing income, expenditure, or prices. What is important is stabilization of the average growth rate over a one- to two-year period at the target level. In both Japan and the United States, the fluctuations of seasonally adjusted narrow money are very large and those of broad money vis-à-vis the same period of the previous year are very small. Thus, in the United States during the early 1980s, the focus on M1 concentrated attention on the indicator with the largest fluctuations, while in Japan attention was focused continuously on the most stable indicator.

Semantics also play a role in Japan. The term "forecast" is used in the announced figures of the Bank of Japan, even though this forecast in fact includes in the calculation the policy behavior of the Bank of Japan itself. This approach implies that the Bank of Japan implicitly accepts the forecast level of the money supply growth rate. To this extent, the forecast values establish policy information that is of significance to the public. The important points are that the trust of the public has been acquired, that the Bank of Japan is controlling the money supply, and that the Bank of Japan has both the ability and the intent to achieve low inflation. Actually establishing targets and announcing them is therefore not at the heart of the matter. As a practical problem, the announcement of targets can also increase political pressure and become potentially dangerous. If, for example, publicized targets were to become related to the public economic forecasts of the government, then monetary policy would be constrained, and collapse of the targets might occur in cases when the government changed its economic forecast. Thus, the Bank of Japan's announcement of only forecast values for money supply growth is sufficient from the point of view of supplying general information about policy.

The monetary aspect of macroeconomic stability
Let us once again briefly summarize the monetary policy background to the stabilization of macroeconomic performance in Japan between 1975 and 1985. First, the Bank of Japan focused attention on the long-term growth rates of the broad money supply, that is, on year-on-year growth rates, the indicator of which growth rates are the most stable not only in Japan but in other countries as well. Second, the Bank of Japan succeeded to the extent shown in Figure 1 in stabilizing money growth. The Bank thus emphasized that money supply growth trends that were stable and at an appropriate level would not allow an outbreak of homemade inflation to occur even if, for example, increases in oil prices had one-shot effects of raising the prices of energy or energy-related products. As can be seen in Figure 1, this was the actual course of events at the time of the second oil crisis. In 1980, the year just after the second oil crisis, inflation as measured by the GNP deflator remained at only 5 percent, and began to fall as early as 1981. As a result, homemade inflation was avoided, and the view was confirmed that the Bank of Japan had both the ability and the intention to maintain price stability. Trust in the Bank of Japan was preserved. Expected inflation has remained at a very low level, and actual inflation

has not deviated from expectations by any significant amount.

At the time of the subsequent, simultaneous, worldwide recession, the Bank of Japan emphasized the strength of Japan's ability to recover equilibrium, that is, the same strength of re-equilibration of firms noted above. The Bank's view was that, to the extent prices were stable, there would be a recovery of stable long-term growth without stimulative fiscal policy or monetary easing. As seen in Figure 1, this was in fact the case by 1984–1985. With money growth of about 7 to 8 percent after 1983 and a contribution to growth from real fiscal expenditure of about 1 to 2 percent since 1983 (the year that fiscal consolidation began), real economic growth recovered to the 5 percent level in 1984, led by the recovery of domestic private demand and balance of payments surpluses.

The Bank of Japan's policy reactions since 1975 have been neither Keynesian discretionary fine-tuning nor a monetarist x-rule, but rather a combination of the two. The reactions have been discretionary in the sense that they sought a gradual reduction in the growth rate of money supply, but they have also followed rules in the sense that they have stabilized money growth to the extent possible and have provided information about policy in the form of announced forecasts of money growth. An appropriate term for this approach is eclectic gradualism.

Control of Money Stock and Its Effect on the Economy

The questions that remain to be asked are how the Bank of Japan can control the monetary growth path with the stability indicated in Figure 1 and how stable the relationship is between monetary growth and macroeconomic performance. These are discussed below.

Control mechanism of money stock

The Bank of Japan controls the money stock through changes in the call and bill rates, which are interbank money rates, as operating variables. The monetary control of the Bank of Japan takes the form of accommodative provision (or absorption) of credit when the demand for high-powered money fluctuates. The Bank of Japan has never adopted the so-called multiplier approach whereby the money supply is indirectly controlled by the direct control of the supply of high-powered money through a stable multiplier relationship.

We estimate a vector autoregressive (VAR) model of three variables, namely, the money stock (M), high-powered money (H), and the short-term money market rate (r), during the period between the first quarter of 1968 and the fourth quarter of 1987. Table 2 reports F statistics on the hypothesis that there was a causal relationship in the sense of Granger. Two things can be seen:

1) There was unidirectional causality from r to M and from r to H, indicating that the control of the short-term money market rates constitutes the first step in the Bank of Japan's conduct of monetary policy.

2) There was unidirectional causality from M to H, indicating the absence of the multiplier approach in Japan's monetary control.

Let us next consider the process by which changes in the call and bill rates ultimately affect the money stock, by taking as an example a case where the Bank of Japan attempts to restrain growth in the money stock. Generally speaking, there are three channels by which changes in the call and bill rates affect the money stock.

First, the increase in the interbank market rates brought about by operations of the Bank of Japan reduces the marginal profitability of additional loans and increases the profitability of portfolio investments on short-term money

Table 2.   F statistics based on three-variable VAR model.

Dependent \ Independent	H	r	M	Causality
H	2.840	6.913*	11.765**	H
r	0.418	318.067**	0.728	r
M	0.103	6.294**	136.347**	M

H: high-powered money;
r: weighted average of call and bill rates;
M: money stock (M2 +CDs).

Source: Bank of Japan, *Economic Statistics Monthly* (seasonally adjusted).
Notes: 1. Period: from the 1st quarter of 1968 to the 4th quarter of 1987.
2. All variables are percentage increases over the previous quarter.
3. Lag length of the estimated VAR model is selected by the minimum AIC.
4. **(*) indicates that the F value is significant at 1(5)%.

market assets for financial institutions. Consequently, financial institutions reduce loans and increase net lendings in the interbank money markets; this follows from the fact that the loan rates of financial institutions are less flexible than the interbank rates because they are significantly influenced by prime lending rates, which are in turn based on regulated deposit rates, and by the consideration of long-term customer relationships. Moreover, the effect of an increase in interbank rates on the amount of loans of financial institutions through this channel is supplemented by so-called window guidance (a type of moral suasion by the Bank of Japan), which is intended to limit the quarterly increases in the total loan volume of individual financial institutions.

Second, an increase in the interbank market rates raises the open money market rates and yields on medium- and long-term government bonds through arbitrage, causing individuals and nonfinancial firms to make portfolio adjustments away from deposits with regulated interest rates to open market instruments and government bonds for which yields have risen. Financial institutions would thus suffer from outflows of funds in deposits with regulated interest rates (viz., financial disintermediation). Along with the development of open money markets and government bond markets, nonbanking sector behavior has important effects upon the money stock via portfolio selection.

Third, an increase in interbank rates reduces the expenditures of the private nonfinancial sector by raising the cost of obtaining loans or issuing bonds. Business firms thus reduce plant or inventory investment and households reduce expenditures on housing or consumer goods. Such a reduction in business and household expenditures gives rise to a slowdown in the nominal value of transactions in the economy as a whole and, as a result, reduces the transactions-motivated component of the demand for money, mainly in the business sector. Moreover, the slowdown of real economic activity influences household savings through a fall in income, thereby reducing the asset-motivated component of the demand for money.

Although these three transmission channels still existed as of 1988, the further liberalization of deposit rates since the spring of 1985 changed the relative importance of each money stock control channel. More recent important liberalization measures have included the introduction of deposits bearing market-related interest rates (MMCs), relaxation of issuing conditions of CDs, and liberalization of the interest rates on large-denomination time deposits. These measures caused a shift of bank loans from traditional "prime rate banking" based on regulated interest rates to "spread banking" based on market interest rates.

These developments are likely to affect each of the three transmission channels. First, proliferation of spread banking will weaken the restraining effect of a reduction in the marginal profitability of loans on the money stock (the first channel). Second, further liberalization of deposit rates will reduce the effect of the so-called disintermediation on the money stock (the second channel) by allowing deposit rates to move in parallel with the short-term money market rates. Third, liberalization of deposit rates and subsequent increases in spread banking in the bank loan market will strengthen the effect of a reduction in the business and household demand for money on the money stock (the third channel).

Therefore, it is impossible to make an *a priori* judgment on whether the recent liberalization of deposit rates has weakened the control mechanism of the money stock. Cross-correlation analysis, however, indicates that the negative correlation between the call rate and the money stock (M2 + CDs) became somewhat smaller and the length of lag longer during the period after 1985, when a series of measures was taken to liberalize deposit rates (Table 3). Of course, there still exists a negative correlation between the short-term interest rate and the money stock, and the Bank of Japan will continue to control the money stock by influencing the call and bill rates. Nevertheless, one must

Table 3. Lagged correlation coefficients between the call rate and the money stock.

	Period	Maximum coefficients	Number of lags
Quarterly data[1]	I/1975 ~ IV/1979	−0.751	− 1
	I/1980 ~ IV/1984	−0.660	− 2
	I/1985 ~ IV/1987	−0.480	− 4
Monthly data[2]	01/1975 ~ 12/1979	−0.455	− 3
	01/1980 12/1984	−0.451	− 5
	01/1985 ~ 01/1988	−0.350	−18

Source: Bank of Japan, *Economic Statistics Monthly* (seasonally adjusted).
Notes: 1. Percentage increases over the previous quarter.
        2. Percentage increases over the previous month.

watch very carefully how rapidly financial liberalization measures will change the way money stock control is effected in Japan.

Relationship between money stock and real economic activity

The reason why the Bank of Japan has been paying close attention to the broadly defined money stock as an intermediate target of monetary policy lies in the existence of a stable relationship between the broad money stock and several real economic variables, as has been demonstrated by many empirical studies. In particular, the stable relationship that exists between the money stock and the price level, which is the ultimate objective of the Bank of Japan, is an important background factor in the monetary targeting policy.

Let us now review the relationship between the money stock and real economic activity by estimating a VAR model. First, we estimate the VAR model of four variables, high-powered money (H), the short-term interest rate (r), the money stock (M), and nominal GNP (Y), during the period from the second quarter of 1967 to the fourth quarter of 1987 (Table 4). F statistics indicate unidirectional causality, in the sense of Granger, running from M to Y, but show no evidence of causality running from r to H or from H to Y. These results reconfirm the importance of the money stock as an intermediate target. Furthermore, the evidence of three sets of unidirectional causality, i.e., from r to M, from r to H, and from M to H, is identical to the causal relationships observed in the earlier three-variable VAR model and seems to confirm the validity of our hypothesis about the working mechanism of Japan's money market: the Bank of Japan controls the money stock by influencing short-term interest rates and providing (or ab-

Table 4.   F statistics based on four- and five-variable VAR models.

1. Four-variable VAR model for H, r, M, and Y

Ind. Dep.	H	r	M	Y	Causality
H	1.808	7.551**	7.372**	0.719	
r	0.028	248.384**	0.982	2.187	
M	0.143	6.152**	113.770**	0.089	
Y	0.531	1.264	9.232**	3.549*	

2. Five-variable VAR model for H, r, M, y, and P

Ind. Dep.	H	r	M	y	P	Causality
H	1.063	9.121**	8.095**	0.409	1.957	
r	0.002	191.293**	0.696	0.894	2.331	
M	0.302	5.279**	108.287**	0.247	0.805	
y	0.182	0.163	3.825*	1.028	3.419*	
P	0.173	1.419	7.832**	1.061	21.110**	

3. Five-variable VAR Model for r, M, y, P, and s

Ind. Dep.	r	M	y	P	s	Causality
r	117.146**	0.409	0.277	2.741*	6.204**	
M	5.801**	26.495**	0.946	0.555	0.911	
y	0.277	5.589*	3.637*	5.915**	0.080	
P	0.745	6.048**	1.957	25.346**	0.802	
s	0.150	0.207	0.122	0.315	4.185*	

H: High-powered money; r: weighted average of call and bill rates; M: money stock (M+CDs); Y: nominal GNP; y: real GNP; P: GNP deflator; s: exchange rate.

Notes: 1. Period: from the 1st quarter of 1968 to the 4th quarter of 1987 in cases 1 and 2; from the 2nd quarter of 1973 to the 2nd quarter of 1988 in case 3.

2. All variables are percentage increases over the previous quarter.

3. Lag length of the estimated VAR model is selected by the minimum AIC.

4. **(*) indicates that F-value is significant at 1 (5)% in cases 1 and 2 and 1 (10)% in case 3.

sorbing) central bank credit to accommodate fluctuations in the demand for high-powered money.

Next, we estimate a VAR model with five variables, by adding real GNP (y), in place of nominal GNP (Y), and GNP deflator (P) to the four-variable VAR model (Table 4). F statistics indicate the presence of three sets of unidirectional causality, running from M to P, from M to y, and from P to y. The causality from P to y suggests the so-called deflationary effect of inflation, implying that an increase in M might have two results that largely offset each other: an increase in y and the deflationary effect of inflation. As a result, the effect of an increase in M on y is uncertain in the long run and the long-run Phillips curve is nearly vertical. This is evidence that, as discussed above, the Japanese economy can be assumed not to deviate much from the vertical long-run Phillips curve. Furthermore, it should be noted here that the causal relationships among three variables, H, r, and M, are the same as those in the three- or four-variable VAR model.

Finally, in order to investigate the transmission mechanism of the effect of monetary policy in an open macroeconomy, we estimate another VAR model of five variables, by adding exchange rate (s) in place of high-powered money (H) to the above VAR model (Table 4). In an open macroeconomy with floating exchange rates, it is usually considered that causality runs from r to s, and then from s to y through changes in exports and/or imports. However, our results for the estimated VAR model show no causality from r to s or from s to y, but they show a reverse causality from s to r. Here it should be added that the causal relationships among r, M, p, and y are nearly the same as those in the above-indicated closed economy model.

How should we interpret the causality from s to r in an open macro-economy model of Japan? First, since the advent of the floating exchange rate system, the yen-dollar

exchange rate has moved exogenously rather than endoge-
nously for the Japanese economy. The first and second oil
shocks caused depreciation of the yen; the high U.S. interest rates in the first half of the 1980s brought some appreciation of the dollar, but this trend has been reversed
by the international policy coordination among leading industrial countries since the Plaza Accord of September
1985. The Bank of Japan has reacted to the yen's depreciation (or appreciation) by raising (reducing) short-term
interest rates. In other words, the estimated causality from
s to r indicates the reaction function of the Bank of Japan
to the exogenous movements in foreign exchange markets.

Second, the Bank of Japan recognizes the effect of interest rate policy upon exchange rates and has sometimes
manipulated short-term interest rates in order to rectify
the misalignment of exchange rates, as it did for example
with the sharp rises of interest rates in 1982 and 1985. However, the effect of this type of active interest rate policy on
the exchange rate objectives has been overwhelmed, on
the average, by that of defensive interest rate policy generated by the Bank of Japan's reaction function.

The remaining question is why there exists no relationship between s and y. Although the yen's appreciation
(depreciation) has brought about either decreased (increased) current-account surpluses or increased (decreased)
deficits, there have been offsetting changes in domestic
demand. We understand that the falls (or rises) in short-
term interest rates have contributed to the increases (or
decreases) in domestic demand. That is to say, we have
experienced a kind of reswitching between external and
domestic demand, and the economy always follows the
stable growth path in line with the stable growth of supply
capacity. This was already discussed earlier in this chapter,
and Figure 2 was given as evidence.

Stability of the demand for money function

Having analyzed the mechanism of money stock control and the relationships between the money stock and real economic activity, let us now investigate the recent stability of the demand for money function, which summarizes the functional relationship of the money stock with short-term interest rates and real economic variables. Here, as a standard specification, we assume that the real money stock is determined by short-term interest rate and real GNP. Estimation of a standard money demand function based on the data during the period from the third quarter of 1978

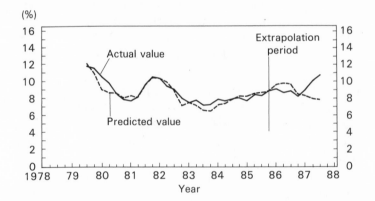

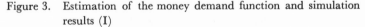

Figure 3. Estimation of the money demand function and simulation results (I)

Notes: 1. Estimated function: period III/78–IV/85

$$\ln(M/P) = -1.3257 + 0.2260 \ln(Y/P) - 0.2732 \ln(1+r)$$
$$\quad\quad (2.1) \quad\quad\quad\quad (4.9)$$
$$+ 0.8544 \ln(M/P)_{-1} + \varepsilon$$
$$(12.6)$$

$R^2 = 0.999$ and S.E. $= 0.00469$.

D.W. $= 1.946$, and t values are in parentheses.

M, M_2 + CDs (average outstanding, seasonally adjusted); Y, nominal GNP; P, GNP deflator; r, *gensaki* (repurchase) rate.

2. Extrapolation is done as a dynamic simulation beginning in the 4th quarter of 1985.

to the fourth quarter of 1985 yields a good fit (Figure 3). If we use the estimated function to extrapolate, we can satisfactorily trace the actual path of the money stock from the first quarter of 1986 until the fourth quarter of 1986. However, the estimated function substantially underforecasts the actual path of the money stock after 1987. Therefore, the standard demand for money function does not explain the sharp increases in money stock growth after 1987.

Next, we estimate an alternatively specified demand for

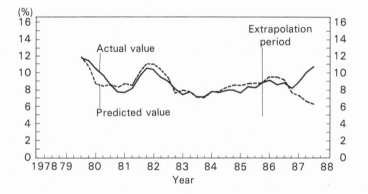

Figure 4.   Estimation of the money demand function and simulation results (II)

Notes: 1. Estimated function: period III/78–IV/85

$$\ln(M/P) = -0.9967 + 0.1772 \ln(Y/P) - 0.3741 \ln(1+c)$$
$$\qquad\qquad (1.5) \qquad\qquad\qquad (4.2)$$
$$\qquad + 0.8815 \ln(P/M)_{-1} + \varepsilon$$
$$\qquad (12.1)$$

where $R^2 = 0.999$ and S.E. $= 0.00504$.

D.W. $= 1.895$, and t values are in parentheses.

M, $M_2 + CDs$; Y, nominal GNP; P, GNP deflator; c, opportunity cost for holding $M_2 + CDs$ [(*gensaki* rate)-(Average yield on $M_2 + CDs$)].

2. Extrapolation is done as a dynamic simulation beginning in the 4th quarter of 1985.

money function by employing the difference between the weighted average of interest rates on individual components of M2 + CDs and the money market interest rate, in place of the money market interest rate itself. This specification takes into account the possibility that the increased weight of free market instruments in M2 + CDs has reduced the opportunity cost for holding M2 + CDs; for example, the share of free market instruments in M2 + CDs increased from 8.6% in December 1985 to 19.5% in October 1987. According to the estimated results, however, the modified version shows little improvement over the standard demand for money function (Figure 4).

The empirical analysis above indicates that the post-1987 sharp increase in the money growth rate in Japan cannot be well explained by the demand for money function. At first glance, such a phenomenon seems to suggest the instability of the demand for money function. However, the under-prediction of the money stock might have been caused by the shift in the money supply function. For example, short-term and long-term interest rates have recently declined to extremely low levels by historical standards and, as a result, the prices of existing assets, such as land and stocks, have increased significantly. Accordingly, the ability of the nonfinancial sector to borrow has risen with the increase in the value of collateral; the financial sector has increased lending activity. If this interpretation is correct, we have an identification problem. Thus, it is very difficult to know whether the function we are estimating is the "demand for money" function or the "supply of money" function, because both functions could be specified in almost the same way.

Another way of interpreting the sharp increase in the money growth rate in Japan is to take the stock-motivated demand for money component into consideration. That is, the post-1987 increase in the stock of wealth, such as the values of stock shares and real estates, might have contributed to the increase in the demand for money. If that is the case, the money demand function, which includes the stock of wealth as an additional explanatory variable, could solve the problem of the recent under-prediction of the money stock.

As already described, the mechanism of money stock control has been changing under the liberalization of deposit rates; the ability of the standard demand for money function to forecast a future money stock has been declining. Therefore, we must pay careful attention to further changes in the money stock control mechanism and in the forecasting ability of the money demand function in the conduct of monetary targeting policy in Japan in the future.

Macroeconomic Performance in Five Countries under the Floating Exchange Rate System

In concluding this chapter, I would like to point out the similar experiences of price stability and stable growth in other countries under the floating exchange rate system. International observations of macroeconomic performance in five leading industrialized countries under the floating exchange system are detailed below.

Similar stabilities in international observations
The complete breakdown of the Bretton Woods system occurred in 1973, and floating exchange rates have since been the rule in the major industrialized countries. In comparing the macroeconomic performance of these five countries before and after the system changed, three major characteristics are recognized. First, macroeconomic fluctuations in the five countries have become simultaneous. Second, the macroeconomies of the countries have in some cases and respects become less stable. As shown in Table 5, the trend inflation rates of the G-5 countries have risen since

Table 5.   Trends and deviations of economic indicators before and after the shift to floating exchange rates (in percentages).

	Mean trend			Standard deviation of trend		
	1954/I –72/IV (A)	75/I –86/IV (B)	(B) – (A)	1954/I –72/IV (A)	75/I –86/IV (B)	(B) – (A)
Japan						
Real growth	9.39	4.15	–	3.12	0.93	–
Unemployment	1.59	2.27	+	0.19	0.14	–
Consumer price inflation	4.70	5.43	+	2.12	1.55	–
Current account/GNP	0.24	1.23	+	0.86	0.98	+
United States						
Real growth	3.01	3.01	0	2.57	3.00	+
Unemployment	4.94	7.41	+	0.78	1.11	+
Consumer price inflation	2.44	7.09	+	0.57	0.80	+
Current account/GNP	0.42	–0.85	–	0.25	0.62	+
United Kingdom						
Real growth	2.36	2.36	0	1.87	2.36	+
Unemployment	2.08	7.45	+	0.25	0.37	+
Consumer price inflation	5.11	10.17	+	1.33	4.77	+
Current account/GNP	–0.25	0.12	+	0.97	1.57	+

Federal Republic of Germany						
Real growth	4.38	2.00	−	2.61	2.32	−
Unemployment	0.97	6.27	+	0.27	0.33	+
Consumer price inflation	2.91	3.80	+	1.56	1.34	−
Current account/GNP	2.13	2.34	+	0.85	0.81	−
France						
Real growth	4.64	2.43	−	2.54	1.57	−
Unemployment	2.52	7.17	+	0.17	0.28	+
Consumer price inflation	5.00	9.77	+	1.58	1.02	−
Current account/GNP	−0.19	−0.25	−	0.58	1.18	+

Note: Figures are the means and standard deviations of the trends, computed using Bayesian techniques. "A" and "B" refer, respectively, to the fixed and floating exchange rate periods. Because of the unavailability of data, the starting time of (A) varies slightly by country and indicator. The quarters from 73/I to 74/IV are omitted in order to abstract from the transitional effects caused by the shift to the new exchange rate system.

the move to floating exchange rates, and major instabilities in performance have emerged, such as the large fluctuations in inflation and real growth rates seen in the United States and the United Kingdom. In Japan, the Federal Republic of Germany, and France, the trend of real growth rates has fallen relative to earlier levels. As a result, the overall growth rate for the G-5 countries has fallen to the relatively lower level of the United States and the United Kingdom. This is one of the background factors behind the across-the-board increase in the unemployment rates in these countries.

One exception to the instability of performance is that in Japan, the Federal Republic of Germany, and France, where real growth rates and inflation rates fluctuated somewhat less, judging from standard deviation of trend in Table 5. In that sense their macroeconomic performance was more stable. Japan's experiences discussed above are not unique, but common in international observations of the countries insofar as their monetary control was successful.

The third characteristic, which emerged in the 1980s, is the trend toward dispersion of current account balances among Japan, the Federal Republic of Germany, and the United States.

These three characteristics of economic performance among the five countries since the advent of floating rates are precisely the opposite of what economic theory had conceived for such a system. According to the theoretical conception, simultaneity of economic fluctuations among the countries would be reduced because of an increase in the independence of macroeconomic policies. In addition, the various national economies would be more stable because the exchange rate could absorb economic disturbances emanating from abroad. Nor would there be trend dispersions of current account balances because of the inherent self-adjustment mechanism attributed to the floating rate system.

Of these differences between theoretical prediction and fact, the first and the second—that is, the simultaneity of macroeconomic fluctuations and the instability—do not go to the heart of the character of the floating rate system and in this sense do not constitute errors in the economic theory of floating rates. Rather, the simultaneous fluctuation and instability have resulted from common shocks from abroad and from policy reactions to them. In contrast, the third characteristic, trend dispersions from current account balance, points out an inadequacy in the theory posited before 1973, which said that such imbalances would be automatically eliminated under the floating rate system.

The common shocks that hit the industrial economies since 1973 have of course been the first (1973–1974) and second (1979–1980) oil crises. Immediately after these shocks, the industrial countries were faced with a "trilemma," that is, an increase in inflation rates, a fall in real growth, and imbalances in current accounts. As a result, the macro-performance among the economies became simultaneous and unstable. In response to the second oil shock, the major industrial countries centered their policies on monetary targeting and adopted a concerted disinflationary policy, thus bringing the average inflation rates down substantially. At the same time, however, a worldwide recession occurred around 1982, and once again macroeconomic performance became simultaneous and unstable.

The oil crises were not of course a result of the floating exchange rate system. Under the Bretton Woods system of fixed exchange rates, the inflation rates of the major industrial countries had gradually accelerated, and the prices of primary commodities relative to industrial commodities had slowly fallen. One result of this trend was the cartel behavior of OPEC and the increase in oil prices. Rather, the major reason for the breakdown of the system was the continuous oversupply of the key currency, the U.S. dollar, without a decrease in its value. This oversupply skewed international balance-of-payments relationships and raised the worldwide inflation rate. In a sense, these difficulties were traceable to the very character of the fixed exchange rate system. In fact, the fixed exchange rate system had already broken down before the first oil crisis because of the same acceleration of inflation that encouraged OPEC. But even if the system had survived somewhat longer, the first oil crisis would have destroyed it completely. The ability of the world economy to adjust to huge supply shocks such as the quadrupling of oil prices after the first oil crisis or the tripling after the second was due only to the previous shift to floating exchange rates and the flexibility of those rates under that system.

Another reason for the judgment that the simultaneous movements and instabilities of the world economy are not due to the floating rate system lies in the differences between Japan, the Federal Republic of Germany, and France on the one hand and the United States and the United Kingdom on the other. These differences show that their degrees of economic stability had changed to opposite directions in some respects since the shift to floating rates. As stated above and shown in Table 5, in the former three countries, the fluctuations of real economic growth and inflation in fact decreased after the second half of the 1970s. The latter two countries saw larger fluctuations and a decrease in their macro-stability.

Among the many reasons for this phenomenon, the differences in economic policy background were important. Concerning monetary policy, in the former three countries, either the money supply growth rate or the real long-term interest rate, or both, saw lower fluctuations while in the latter two countries one or both saw larger fluctuations. In terms of fiscal policy, the fluctuations of fiscal deficits to GNP became particularly large for the latter two countries. It would seem that the management of macroeconomic policy in the three former countries, particularly Japan and the Federal Republic of Germany, obeyed policy rules such as keeping money supply targets and implementing fiscal consolidation, and that through these rules a more stable outcome was achieved. In contrast, in the latter two countries, discretionary policies continued to be repeated. The emergence of such differences in policy management across countries could happen only because of the independence of policies possible after the move to the floating rate system. In this sense, economic theory was correct. The advent of floating rates allowed an interdiction of destabilizing influences among the economies.

Limits of the floating rate system

The expansion of current account imbalances. The essential point of difference between fact and theory concerning the floating rate system was, as discussed above, the emergence of trend imbalances in foreign payments during the 1980s. After the shift to floating rates, the financial and capital markets of different countries became further integrated. As a result, the quantities of foreign exchange trading that accompanied international capital movements became overwhelmingly larger than the amount of foreign exchange trading that accompanied current payments such as those for trade in goods and services. Therefore the short-term foreign exchange market movements came to reflect more strongly the result of these currency trades that accompanied capital movements, and exchange rates themselves took on more of the character of the price of financial assets. Over the long run, of course, purchasing power parity continued to play the role of anchor for the system and to prevent large deviations of exchange rates from the implied purchasing power levels.

Nevertheless, there is no certainty that exchange rates

determined over the short term as financial prices or those determined over the long term by purchasing power parity will be at a level that guarantees balance of current accounts. The sole mechanism that links the exchange market and the current account balance is the accumulation of net foreign asset or liability positions. Through the risks of holding such positions, the movements of exchange rates are constrained, and extreme current account imbalances are not permitted. However, it is extremely difficult to determine the levels at which exchange rates will deter the emergence of such payments imbalances.

In fact, the current account imbalances under the floating exchange rate system are similar to those under the fixed rate system in that they are determined to a considerable extent by domestic absorption, which is strongly affected by the fiscal deficit. The expansion of the current payments imbalances between Japan and the Federal Republic of Germany on one hand and the United States on the other during the 1980s can be related to the fact that the former two countries had ratios of fiscal deficits to GNP that were being reduced on trend through fiscal consolidation while the United States saw the active fiscal policies of the Reagan administration reflected in a trend increase of the fiscal deficit ratios.

The decline of economic growth rates. Among the indicators of macroeconomic performance for the major countries, the movement without a clear relationship to the advent of the floating rate system is the decline of economic growth rates in three of the G-5 economies, that is, Japan, the Federal Republic of Germany, and France. It is clear that international resource allocation may be worse under the floating rate system, judging from such factors as the stimuli to protectionism in the deficit countries, the emergence of voluntary export restraints in those with surpluses, and the increased uncertainty about exchange rate trends associated with repeated overshooting and undershooting of exchange rates over the medium term from levels that would be consistent with purchasing power parity. The associated reductions in economic efficiency were probably one reason for the reduced level of economic growth. However, not all of the G-5 countries saw a reduction in economic growth. In fact Japan, the Federal Republic of Germany, and France, the relatively high-growth countries, saw reductions in the average growth rate while the United States and the United Kingdom, the relatively low-growth countries, saw growth continue at previous levels. Therefore, although there may be a relationship between the reduction of overall growth and the shift to the floating exchange rate system, it is necessary to pay attention to other factors in describing the differences among countries.

The causes of lower growth in Japan, the Federal Republic of Germany, and France may, at least partially, be summarized as follows. First, at the end of the Second World War, these three countries were more damaged and, in some respects, less advanced technologically than were the United States and the United Kingdom, and therefore the growth rates of the former three had a tendency to slow toward those of the latter two as this gap was closed. Second, the industrial countries faced a worsening of the terms of trade because of the two oil crises. Third, there was also an increase in real interest rates around the world in the wake of the expansion of the United States fiscal deficit in the 1980s and the crowding-out effects that it spread across the globe.

Of these three reasons for lower growth, the second and the third also would appear to apply to the United States and the United Kingdom. However, because the United Kingdom had North Sea oil, its terms of trade did not deteriorate so badly. In the case of the United States, the expansion of the current account deficit acted as an increase in overall supply while the expansion of the fiscal deficit acted as an increase in overall demand; thus, the supply effects of the worsening of the terms of trade (the second reason) and the demand effects of the rise in real interest rates (the third reason) were more or less offset.

The reason why the United States was able to maintain growth in the face of these twin deficits was that the American dollar was the world's key currency. Such a situation, however, cannot continue because the world's key currency country is now also the world's largest debtor country. The international currency and financial system has become extremely unstable. This is why the major industrial countries are being forced to restructure the world economic order and to rethink the international currency and financial systems from the point of view of international policy cooperation. We shall discuss these issues further in Part II of this book.

2

The High-Yen Recession and Revival of Stable Growth since 1985

Despite the stable trend after 1974, which was discussed in Chapter 1, the Japanese economy was hit by one external shock that was larger than those experienced before: the enormous appreciation of the yen and depreciation of the dollar after the Plaza Accord of September 1985, an agreement among the finance ministers and central bank governors of the G-5 countries who met at the Plaza Hotel in New York.

The exchange value of the yen vis-à-vis the U.S. dollar bottomed out in February 1985 at about ¥260 per dollar and rose slightly thereafter to reach about ¥240 per dollar in September of that year. With the announcement of the Plaza Accord, however, there was a sharp increase in the value of the yen; by July of 1986, the yen had reached the ¥150–¥160 per dollar level. This represented an appreciation of more than 70 percent from the lowest 1985 value of the yen, and an appreciation of some 60 percent during the 10 months from the time of the Plaza Accord. (These figures correspond to a depreciation of the dollar of more than 40 percent and a bit less than 40 percent, respectively.)

In the 25 months that followed, the appreciation of the yen slowed. During the course of 1988 it fluctuated by amounts of plus or minus ¥7 from the ¥130 per dollar level. That is an appreciation of about 20 percent for the 25 months from July 1986, compared with 60 percent for the 10 months beginning September 1985. We must examine the basic reasons for these trends of the exchange rate; in the subsequent section, we will consider the impact of such fluctuations on the Japanese economy.

Why the Yen Appreciated after the Plaza Accord

The reasons for the large appreciation of the yen and depreciation of the dollar in the period between the Plaza Accord of September 1985 and July of the succeeding year must be explained in a manner that is consistent with the reasons for the strength of the dollar and weakness of the yen in the first years of the 1980s. The major reason for the sharp increase in both the nominal and real values of the U.S. dollar in the first half of the 1980s was a sizable increase in real interest rates that accompanied the policy mix adopted by the Reagan Administration. This was a mix of an expansionary fiscal policy to stimulate economic activities, resulting in large government deficits, and a tight monetary policy to dampen inflation. Both an increase in government financing demand and monetary tightening raised real interest rates in the United States.

In addition, the following factors are thought by market participants to have contributed. First was the view that the U.S. economy would bounce back under the influence of Reaganomics, a view that led to the expectation of a high marginal profit for capital which could sustain investment in such an environment of high interest rates. Second, although the balance of payments deficits of the

United States had accumulated and put the U.S.A. into the position of a debtor nation by the middle of 1985, many market participants did not view this as a major source of dollar weakness. A third and related point is that the market participants did not sufficiently consider the risk premium associated with dollar holdings.

Let us now look at how these four reasons for the strength of the dollar in the early 1980s were reversed after the Plaza Accord of September 1985, and how they became sources of dollar weakness and yen strength.

Change in the policy mix

In the early 1980s, the Reagan Administration stimulated business conditions with an expansionary fiscal policy and resultant large government deficits, but it also established monetary targets and the objective of conquering inflation with contractionary monetary policy through maintaining these targets. That is, the administration adopted an expansionary fiscal policy and a contractionary monetary policy as its policy mix. In the communiqué from the Plaza Accord, however, this stance was reconsidered. The basic thrust of the communiqué was as follows: the high interest rates which followed from the adopted policy mix had brought capital inflows from Japan and Europe, thus strengthening the dollar and weakening parts of the American economy. Therefore, in order to correct the high interest rates, the policy mix that was causing these high rates would be reconsidered; that is, the fiscal deficit would be reduced over a series of years, while on the other hand monetary policy would move toward loosening. After the Plaza Accord, movements were seen that lent credibility to this new stance. The Gramm-Rudman-Hollings Amendment, which dealt with fiscal policy, was proposed by the Republican administration and passed with the cooperation of the opposition party, the Democrats, who held a majority in the House of Representatives. In this law there was a clear policy goal of eliminating fiscal deficits over the subsequent several years.

Monetary policy, in contrast, allowed money growth to exceed the upper limits of target values, and interest rates began to decline. In addition to the declines of market interest rates, there were four cuts in the official discount rate during 1986 by a total of two percentage points, and these cuts further directed market rates lower. Japan also cut its official discount rate three times in the months up to April 1986 for a total of 1.5 percentage points, but, despite this, the interest differentials between Japan and the United States shrank. The differential in long-term interest rates between the United States and Japan had shrunk from 5 percent or more in the period before the Plaza Accord to only about 2 percent by the spring of 1986. The result was a decline in the strength of the capital outflows from Japan to the United States: the foreign exchange market therefore began to move in the direction of a stronger yen and a weaker dollar.

Changed perceptions of U.S. economic strength
Until the September 1985 G-5 meeting in New York, it was thought that Reagan Administration policies would revive the American economy and that, as a result, the profitability of investment in the United States was quite high. Thus, there was a tendency to invest in the United States because it was thought that purchasing capital in the U.S. economy would give a high rate of return. The most important factor in this attitude was certainly the fact that the U.S. economy in 1984 recorded a real growth rate of 6.4 percent. Ironically, in the G-5 statement from the Plaza meeting the U.S. government itself denied this.

The logic of the communiqué was as follows: a strong U.S. economy has not brought with it high interest rates and a strong dollar; rather, these high interest rates and the dollar's strength were weakening the U.S. economy as industries in the United States lost international competitiveness. Protectionism within the country was being encouraged, which was viewed as an alarming development. In the words of the communiqué itself: "The Ministers and Governors agreed that. . . some further orderly appreciation of the main non-dollar currencies against the dollar is desirable. They stand ready to cooperate more closely to encourage this when to do so would be helpful." The prime message of the communiqué was that the causal relationships were the reverse of those in the theory that the strong American economy had created a strong dollar and high interest rates; the communiqué said that this was not true, that high interest rates and the strong dollar had in fact weakened the American economy. As a result of this approach, the people who had invested in the United States based on the image of a strong, reviving American economy became extremely worried. They began to hedge their dollar positions with forward sales, or to sell dollars outright in spot markets. As a result, the value of the dollar fell precipitously.

Recognition of accumulation of debt
The third factor behind the dollar decline was a reconsideration on the part of market participants of the seriousness of the accumulation of foreign debt in the United States and of the current account deficits. The United States became a net debtor sometime in the middle of 1985, and had a total net debt position of about $368 billion by the end of 1987, thus becoming the world's largest debtor country. Moreover, its balance in net investment income moved to the deficit side of the ledger in 1988; turning the current account deficit into a surplus will become much harder, and this net debtor position may well last into the decade of the 1990s.

The amount of the U.S. net deficit position is like an effluent: the risk can neither be hedged nor avoided. Therefore, if large amounts of dollars, for which the risks cannot be covered through hedging and cannot be avoided, are continually spread throughout the world, then in the medium term there will inevitably be a weakening of the dollar. This idea became a strong belief on the part of market participants including corporations and banks, and contributed to the weakening of the dollar and strengthening of the yen.

Flight from the dollar
The fourth reason for the dollar decline reflects the first three but increases their scope; this is the increase in the risk premium associated with holding dollars. The dollar is the world's sole key currency and is the most convenient currency to use in international settlements. If one has excess dollars and wishes to invest them at high interest rates, one need only go to New York to put them in the truly convenient New York dollar markets. Thinking along these lines, there were those who before the G-5 meeting in New York were not concerned about a dollar fall, thinking that there were no other international currencies as convenient as the dollar, so that even if excess dollars were to come to the market, there would be no other place to put them except in New York; therefore, the dollar would not fall.

In fact, however, looking at the actual decline of the dollar after the Plaza Accord, such investors began to think it was dangerous to hold open positions in dollars. Because in fact the dollar had lost so much of its value vis-à-vis the yen, it would be dangerous to invest in dollar-denominated assets without a somewhat higher interest rate that would take into account the potential for such risks. These investors saw clearly that it was dangerous to jump into high-interest dollar assets without subtracting this so-called risk premium.

They therefore required discounts on the dollar, and this constituted the fourth source of pressure on its value.

In fact it was a mistake to believe that the dollar was so convenient a currency that there was nowhere for investors to flee. Some might have thought that the flight into yen or Deutsche-marks and the attempt to settle international payments in yen or marks might fail because of refusal by the counterparts in such transactions to accept those currencies. Some people might also have felt there were inconveniences in working through the Tokyo or Frankfurt markets using yen or marks. Based on such misconceptions, they felt that flight from the dollar was unlikely, that there was no alternative to the dollar, and that therefore large dollar sales would not occur or would not cause a weakening of the dollar.

A flight from the dollar into yen, however, does not necessarily imply selling dollars and converting them into yen. It would be sufficient to use forward contracts to sell the dollar forward and buy yen, thereby covering the dollar risk. When the time for settlement came, dollars could in fact be delivered but at the spot market rate at that time; spot-market dollars could be bought back and at the same time forward-market dollars sold once again in a chain of hedging transactions. Through such transactions, one can continuously hold a spot dollar position and not flee into yen. However, because a fall of the dollar is feared, dollar holdings will be continuously sold in the forward market.

If all investors begin such chain-forward operations, then, even though dollars continue to be held on a balance sheet in a statistical sense, the value of the dollar in the market will fall precipitously. This is because the forward market will show continuous pressure for dollar sales; as the forward market for the dollar falls, the interest parity relationship between U.S. and Japanese interest rates will require a reduction in the spot dollar value as well.

The tendency to hold uncovered, dollar-denominated assets without considering risk was therefore reconsidered after it became clear that the dollar had fallen and that the profitability of dollar investments must include a risk premium. The degree of that risk is generally based on the degree to which the current value deviates from the long-term anchor of purchasing power parity.

Slowing Down of the Yen Appreciation after July 1986

The previous section summarized the reasons for the sharp rise of the yen and fall of the dollar between the Plaza Accord in September 1985 and July 1986. These reasons for yen strength and dollar weakness can be restated as follows. The first was the reversal after the Plaza Accord of the real interest rate differentials that accompanied changes in the savings and investment balances (the original reason for which was the policy mix of the Reagan administration). Second was the movement to the net debtor position of the United States (the risk factor). Third was the disappearance of the misconceptions about the U.S. economy and the U.S. dollar. The result was the reversal of deviations of the dollar from purchasing power parity rates and the return of the dollar toward the long-term anchor caused by flight from the U.S. currency.

These views are confirmed by an empirical analysis by Dr. Mitsuhiro Fukao, senior economist of the Institute for Monetary and Economic Studies of the Bank of Japan, which is summarized in Figures 5-a and 5-b. In Figure 5-a, one can observe that the yen-dollar real exchange rate, the deviation of the yen-dollar rate from its purchasing power parity, has risen substantially since 1985, together with an increase in Japan's accumulated current balances

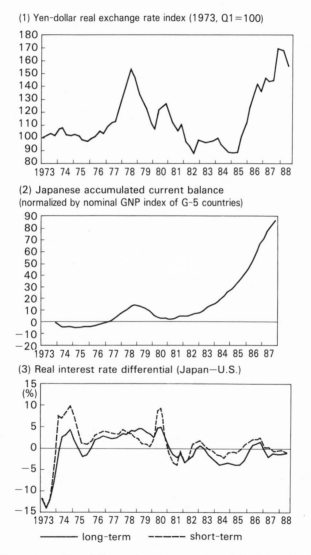

(1) Yen-dollar real exchange rate index (1973, Q1=100)

(2) Japanese accumulated current balance
(normalized by nominal GNP index of G-5 countries)

(3) Real interest rate differential (Japan—U.S.)

———— long-term   —————— short-term

Figure 5-a.   Yen-dollar real exchange rate and its determinants (the counterpart of U.S. accumulation of net external debt) and a decrease in real interest rate differentials between Japan and the United States. In Figure 5-b, this yen-dollar real exchange rate is estimated as a function of the accumulated current balance and the real interest rate differential with the Kalman filter method. The estimated coefficients of these two explanatory variables are shown in Figure 5-b. These two figures confirm the following points. First, both the narrowing of the real interest rate differential and the improvement in Japan's net creditor position (i.e., deterioration in the U.S. net debtor position) can explain, with the usual statistical significance, an appreciation of the yen-dollar real exchange rate (the return of the yen-dollar exchange rate toward its purchasing power parity level) since the Plaza Accord of 1985. Second, as the coefficient β shows, the risk premium on holding dollars in place of yen has been rising since 1985 and was one of the reasons for the appreciation of the yen-dollar real exchange rate after 1985.

Pure economic reasons for yen stability
Two of these three medium-term factors changed after July 1986. The slowdown in the appreciation of the yen for the two-year period after July 1986 had its economic background in this development. Let us reconsider these reasons for yen stability in a somewhat different order.

To begin with, the return to purchasing power parity had almost been completed by 1988. Calculations of purchasing power parity can differ significantly depending on the base period chosen and whether one chooses a GNP deflator or a price index for industrial goods from the wholesale price index. But, as is clear from Figures 6-a and 6-b, any base period after the advent of floating exchange rates (February 1973) will show that a yen-dollar rate of ¥125–¥150 puts the yen nearly at its purchasing power parity

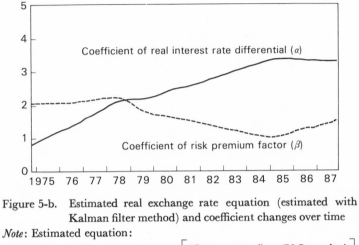

Figure 5-b.   Estimated real exchange rate equation (estimated with Kalman filter method) and coefficient changes over time

Note: Estimated equation:

$$\begin{pmatrix}\text{Yen-dollar real}\\\text{exchange rate}\end{pmatrix} = (\text{Constant}) + \alpha \underbrace{\left[\begin{pmatrix}\text{Japanese real}\\\text{interest rate}\end{pmatrix} - \begin{pmatrix}\text{U.S. real}\\\text{interest rate}\end{pmatrix}\right]}_{\text{Real interest rate differential}}$$

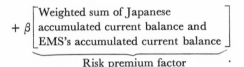

$$+ \beta \underbrace{\left[\begin{array}{l}\text{Weighted sum of Japanese}\\\text{accumulated current balance and}\\\text{EMS's accumulated current balance}\end{array}\right]}_{\text{Risk premium factor}} \cdot$$

rate whether one takes the GNP deflator or any wholesale price deflator for tradable goods, and no matter which time in the 1970s is chosen as the base period. In real terms, the yen is at its strongest level in history. As far as purchasing power parity is concerned, the yen has strengthened sufficiently. From this point of view there was no further reason for the yen to strengthen.

Next, let us consider interest rate differentials. Before the Plaza Accord, the long-term interest differential between the United States and Japan was 5 percent or more. After the Plaza Accord the changes in U.S. and Japanese monetary policy narrowed this differential to 2 percent, but in

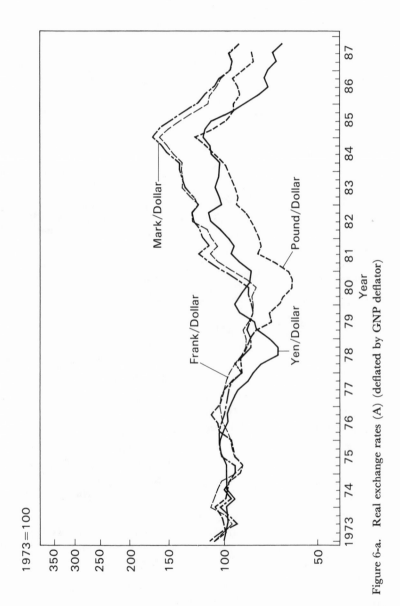

Figure 6-a.   Real exchange rates (A) (deflated by GNP deflator)

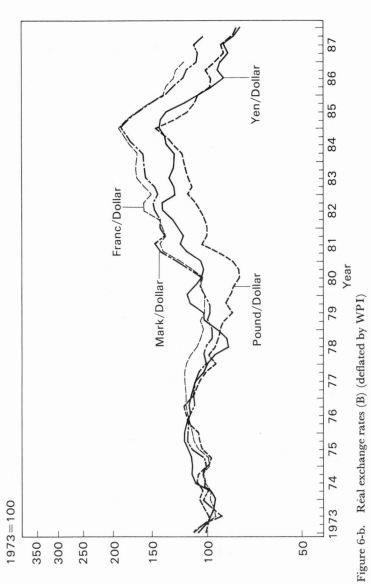

1973=100

Franc/Dollar

Mark/Dollar

Yen/Dollar

Pound/Dollar

Figure 6-b.   Réal exchange rates (B) (deflated by WPI)

1987 the differential expanded once again to about 4 percent. This can be confirmed in Figure 5-a. The movements of interest rates on long-term government bonds in the autumn of 1987 showed that Japanese rates were in the 5 percent range while U.S. rates were in the 9 percent range. Therefore, long-term interest rate differential considerations would not suggest any further reason for yen strengthening. That is, interest rate differentials in 1987 were at about the same levels as they were in the earlier period of dollar strength.

The re-widening of interest rate differentials did in fact begin in the first half of 1987. The atmosphere at that time was that the period of low inflation in the United States was nearing an end, and the markets felt that the inflation rate would rise somewhat toward the end of the year and therefore short-term rates were likely to increase in 1988. Because long-term interest rates depend on a weighted average of current short-term rates and expected short-term rates, long-term interest rates rose with the increase in expected future short-term interest rates. As a matter of fact, the discount rate in the United States was raised twice thereafter, once in September 1987 and again in August 1988. In the meantime, Japan implemented no discount rate change after the final cut to 2.5 percent in February 1987. Long-term rates in Japan remained low in sympathy, and the interest rate differential between the two countries bottomed out at the 2 percent level in early 1987 and widened to around 4 percent through 1988.

Let us finally consider the current account deficit and its accumulation. The trade deficit figures of the United States (published at the time without seasonal adjustment) peaked once at ¥42.8 billion in the third quarter of 1986, a peak that occurred after the Plaza Accord. Between that time and the second quarter of 1987, no higher figure for the trade deficit was announced. In the third quarter of

1987, however, a trade deficit of ￥45.4 billion occurred, but it was attributed to the temporary influence of an increase in oil prices; on a quantity basis, or excluding oil trade, the decrease in the deficits was continuing. The total trade deficit started to decline again, and the figure for the second quarter of 1988 was as low as ￥33.0 billion. The view therefore became more widespread that the large dollar depreciation was working to reduce the U.S. trade deficit.

On the Japanese side, the peak came in November 1986, as measured by the yen-denominated, seasonally adjusted current account surplus. A reduction in the surplus became a trend on the Japanese side as well. This reduction in the yen-denominated surplus meant that the dollar-denominated surplus would move in the same direction once the exchange rates stopped moving. There was a problem of denomination, i.e., that the dollar surplus seemed ever larger even though the yen surplus was shrinking, and this became more pronounced as the yen strengthened and the dollar weakened. However, once the exchange rates stabilized, the trends of the surplus measured in different currencies would go in the same direction. This phenomenon is shown for the trade balance in Figure 7. After the Plaza Accord, the trade surplus on a volume basis shrank continuously beginning in January 1986, but, reflecting the improvement in terms of trade that accompanied the strength of the yen, the surplus continued to expand on a yen basis until May 1986, and was flat on a yen basis until the end of 1986. If these data are converted into dollars, the surplus is even higher than that measured on a yen basis, reflecting the weakness of the dollar. With the lull in the improvement of the terms of trade accompanying the strength of the yen and the weakness of the dollar in early 1987, the declining trend of the surplus on a volume basis was then reflected in both the yen and the dollar value figures, and the surplus began to decline rapidly.

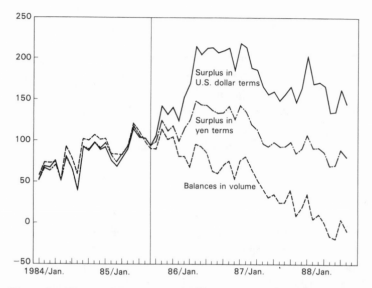

Figure 7.   The trade surplus, 1984–1988 (July-September 1984 = 100)
Notes: 1. Customs clearance base (export-import), seasonally adjusted.
2. Figures for May-December 1986 are adjusted for temporary large increases in gold imports for minting memorial coins.
3. Surplus in yen terms (seasonally adjusted) is calculated by multiplying the exports and imports in dollar terms (seasonally adjusted) by the yen/dollar exchange rate.

Thus, all three medium-term reasons behind the movements of the exchange rates are no longer reasons for further rapid movement of the yen upward or the dollar downward. This is the economic reason for the slowing down in the strengthening of the yen over the medium term since July of 1986.

The political and economic factors

The lull in the appreciation of the yen also had a political background. In the months of October and November 1986 the appreciation of the yen was temporarily reversed slightly to around 160 yen per dollar, but in 1987 appreciation continued, with the yen once again breaking 140 yen per dollar in April and May. In order to prevent such movements toward a yet stronger yen and weaker dollar, Japanese Finance Minister Miyazawa and U.S. Treasury Secretary Baker met in January 1987 and announced their agreement that further strengthening of the yen and weakening of the dollar would not be desirable for Japan, the United States, or the world economy; in order to prevent such yen appreciation and dollar depreciation, the two countries would cooperate in exchange market intervention. In the wake of this agreement, the G-7 (with the exception of Italy) finance ministers and central bank governors met in Paris in February and announced a similar agreement, called the Louvre Accord because of the location of the meeting. This agreement said that further adjustment of current account imbalances would be accomplished not through exchange rate changes in the market such as further yen appreciation or dollar depreciation, but rather through fiscal deficit reduction in the United States and demand expansion in Japan and the Federal Republic of Germany.

This agreement marked an end to the policy cooperation in correcting the value of the dollar based on the Plaza Accord and the beginning of policy cooperation to prevent further dollar weakness based on the Louvre Accord of February 1987. This 180-degree about-face in the purpose of agreement had as background the following three factors.

First, a further decline in the dollar would have engendered even more dollar declines and weakened capital inflows to the United States, with a resulting increase in long-term interest rates. Such an increase could not but lead to weakened economic conditions in the United States in the 1988 presidential election year. Moreover, if dollar weakness invited price increases in world raw materials markets, then inflation would be stimulated. The Reagan Administration wished to avoid at all costs the occurrence of simultaneous inflation and recession—that is, of stagflation—in an election year.

Second, Japan had begun to suffer from a strong yen recession by the start of 1986 and naturally wished to prevent further strengthening of the yen and weakening of the dollar. Even in the Federal Republic of Germany, which had looked with some indifference on these difficulties faced by Japan, the deflationary effects of the stronger Deutschemark gradually rose to the surface, and GNP growth in the fourth quarter of 1986 was negative vis-à-vis the previous quarter, with the outlook for further negative growth in the first quarter of 1987. (The actual figures announced thereafter showed the expected negative growth.) If the Federal Republic of Germany had fallen into a recession, then all of Western Europe would have faced economic constraints. Therefore, all the European G-7 countries agreed to the prevention of further fall of the dollar.

The third factor was the debt crisis. If the United States, Japan, and the Federal Republic of Germany all fell into recession, a simultaneous worldwide recession would ensue and the debtor countries, especially in Latin America, would face increases in interest payments because of the rise in dollar interest rates on their dollar-denominated loans, in addition to stagnation of exports. Both of these developments would hinder the efforts toward economic recovery. As a result, banks in the United States would be hard hit if interest and principal repayments were postponed, with the possibility of generating instabilities in the international monetary system as a whole. Such a development would have been worrisome for the world economy. (This point will be reconsidered in Chapter 3, which compares recent developments with the world depression after 1929.)

These three factors were the basic background for the Louvre Accord. During 1986 U.S. government officials took every possible opportunity to try to "talk down" the dollar, saying that then-current levels of dollar weakness and yen strength were not sufficient, and that it would be desirable for the correction of international payments imbalances that there be further weakening of the dollar and strengthening of the yen. But in 1987 these officials refrained from making such statements. As a result, participants in the foreign exchange markets revised their expectations of further weakness of the dollar and strengthening of the yen and the Deutsche-mark, and the markets brought about a slight strengthening of the dollar and weakening of the yen and the mark around mid-1987. The focal point of international policy cooperation then switched to domestic macroeconomic policies, such as domestic demand expansion and fiscal consolidation, which would directly work on the savings-investment balances in the individual countries.

Indeed, with the United States facing a presidential election in the autumn of 1988, it was highly unlikely that a fiscal deficit reduction program to curtail domestic demand would be seriously considered for 1988. The top priority of the Reagan Administration was to maintain the low unemployment rate and high profit rate of 1987 until the 1988 election. Thus, it feared an outbreak of stagflation not only from inflationary pressures but also from a recession due to a shortage of domestic demand. Therefore, it would not seriously curtail domestic demand in order to reduce the foreign deficit; or, if it did curtail demand, it would only do so when fears of inflation were rising because of strength in domestic business conditions. In an election campaign, the continuation of the foreign deficit might be used as an excuse for "Japan-bashing." To the electorate of the United States, a large country with a low degree of reliance on foreign trade, the foreign deficit itself would not be likely to be a major issue.

A history of policy cooperation
What really happened beginning in the second half of 1988 can be better understood in the context of changes in

policy cooperation at each stage of economic development since the Plaza Accord of September 1985.

In the summer of 1988, decisions were made by the Bundesbank and the Federal Reserve to raise their official discount rates. This clearly marked the end of an era of "cooperative interest rate reductions," leading to the question of whether an era of "cooperative rises" or "noncooperation" will occur subsequently. Actually, neither scenario is likely. Rather, the most likely scenario will still be one of "cooperation," although the aim and content will be different. Cooperation has not always meant "cooperative interest rate reduction": the nature of cooperation changed at least three times after the Plaza Accord of September 1985, and in 1988 we were in the fourth phase.

The first phase was the period between the 1985 Plaza Meeting and the Louvre Accord of February 1987. The Plaza Accord aimed at adjusting the overvalued exchange rate of the U.S. dollar, and therefore the first initiative taken was to bring down high U.S. interest rates, which had been the main cause of the high U.S. dollar. As a result of lowering U.S. interest rates, the differential between long-term interest rates in the United States on one side and those in Europe and Japan on the other, which had exceeded five percentage points before the Plaza Accord, shrank to around two percentage points. This provided room for interest rate cuts in Europe and Japan, and in order to stimulate growth in domestic demand, the United States, Japan, and major European countries reduced their interest rates in a concerted manner while maintaining the two-percentage-point interest rate differential. This was the start of "cooperative interest rate reduction." This concerted action succeeded in achieving global economic recovery. In addition, the narrower interest rate differential between the United States on the one hand and Japan and Europe on the other resulted in a fall of the U.S. dollar, and its external imbalance began to improve.

By February 1987, when the Louvre Accord was agreed upon, it became obvious that a further weakening of the dollar would be destructive for the world economy, and cooperation entered a second phase. The aim of international policy cooperation in that phase was to prevent any further decline in the U.S. dollar. Interest rates were lowered in Japan and Europe and raised in the United States, as a consequence of which the interest rate differential widened to around four percentage points. The nature of policy cooperation in that phase thus ceased to be aimed at the "cooperative reduction of interest rates."

Faced with the crash of stock prices in October 1987, however, the U.S. authorities, in order to prevent panic in financial markets, discontinued raising interest rates and instead eased monetary conditions. This change in policy stance resulted in a further decline of the dollar, and Japan and major European countries had to lower their interest rates to support the dollar. This was the third phase of cooperation, which could be called the "period of renewed cooperative interest rate reduction."

From the beginning of 1988, the negative side of such activities became increasingly obvious. Inflationary expectations mounted worldwide following renewed cooperative interest rate reductions, which might have been somewhat excessive, and policy cooperation entered a fourth phase. This fourth phase merits detailed discussion. The U.S. economy in 1988 was faced with the following two types of risk: i) wage inflation as a result of a decline in unemployment and ii) the fear of renewed widening of trade deficits, mainly due to increased imports. Both fears stemmed from the same origin: namely, against the background of monetary ease since October 1987, domestic demand showed unexpected strength and did not slow down as much as had been expected in the second half of 1988. If these two risks materialized, they would exert downward pressure on the dollar and fuel exchange rate instability. The increase in the U.S. official discount rate in August 1988 was an attempt to nip fears of such risks in the bud, and was a welcome development not only for the United States but also for the global economy as a whole.

The growth of net exports and fixed investment plays a vital role in the U.S. economy, not least in reducing the twin risks mentioned above. It is thus clear that a slowdown in U.S. economic growth should be occasioned through lower household consumption and housing investment, as well as further cuts in the government expenditure. With regard to the latter, however, we must await the directives of the Bush Administration that took office early in 1989. As a result, whether the much-desired slowdown in domestic demand will be realized or not hinges on the development of consumption and housing investment. While the latter has been moderating, partly reflecting higher interest rates, private consumption remains stable against the background of favorable employment growth and a faster tempo of wage increases. As a consequence, total demand maintained its rapid growth, both industrial production and capacity utilization continued to rise, and the unemployment rate remained very low in the middle of 1988. These buoyant demand conditions were reflected in accelerated wage and price increases. Long-term interest rates started to rise in May 1988, mainly reflecting the low 5.4 percent unemployment rate for April, which triggered inflationary expectations. (The rate was later revised to 5.5 percent.) Furthermore, the Federal Reserve nudged short-term interest rates upward. Given this situation, a rise in the official discount rate had generally been viewed as certain, but this expectation faded when the 5.6 percent

May unemployment figure was released in June. However, as the lower unemployment rates of 5.3 percent and 5.4 percent for June and July, respectively, revealed, this rebound was only temporary.

It seems to be widely accepted that the U.S. natural rate of unemployment lies somewhere between 5.5 percent and 6 percent. If this is true, then the unemployment rate has been below its natural rate since June 1988. This is not surprising since the U.S. economy posted 3.4 percent growth in 1987 and 3.8 percent growth in 1988, compared with a generally accepted medium-term growth potential of 2.5–3 percent.

What seems to be of crucial importance for the future of the global economy is whether, and to what extent, the discount rate rise succeeded in decelerating economic growth during the course of 1988, thus exerting curbing effects on wage and price increases and also containing import growth. In the summer of 1988, the exchange market seemed to view the precautionary official discount rise positively. The U.S. dollar showed strength in spite of the above-mentioned risks, which are factors tending to exert downward pressure on it. This strength of the dollar therefore seemed to reflect the market majority's view that the interest rate hike would prevent both a widening of the trade deficit and also the rekindling of inflation.

An appreciation of the U.S. dollar usually moves in tandem with a decline in the dollar prices of international commodities. Contrary to past experience, however, commodity prices, in particular those of grain and nonferrous metals, have remained high due to drought and mine strikes. For European countries, especially the Federal Republic of Germany, this has meant twofold inflationary pressure from the import side. Furthermore, in many European countries, the negative effects of previous measures taken to stimulate domestic demand are becoming increasingly obvious. In the Federal Republic of Germany, the monetary aggregate is growing above the targeted path; in several other countries, especially the United Kingdom and Italy, domestic market conditions for goods and services are excessively tight.

It is against this background that the Federal Republic of Germany and some of its neighbors, as well as the United Kingdom, have raised their interest rates in several steps through the course of 1988. These measures were expected to curb inflation by fulfilling the following three interrelated tasks: to protect the exchange rates of their respective currencies, to contain the growth of money, and to prevent overheating.

In the current fourth phase, policy cooperation does not mean that major economies simply guide interest rates in the same direction. Rather, it means that each individual economy should contribute to the sustained growth of the global economy by maintaining the stability of its own domestic prices in its own way and upon its own responsibility. In other words, international policy cooperation in this phase means harmony, but not necessarily acting in unison.

The High-Yen Recession and the Mechanism for Overcoming It

The movements of exchange rates since the Plaza Accord of September 1985 and the reasons for them have been considered above; now let us look at their macroeconomic effect on the Japanese economy. As is made clear in Figures 1 and 2, the Japanese economy had recovered to a stable growth path of around 5 percent in 1984 (5.1 percent) and 1985 (4.9 percent), but because of the external shock of yen appreciation, growth in 1986 fell to 2.5 percent. The depth of this trough was greater than that after the second oil crisis of 1981–1982. Fortunately, however, business conditions revived significantly as 1987 began. In calendar year 1987 the real growth rate of the Japanese economy was 4.7 percent, and it accelerated after the third quarter of 1987. The growth rate for fiscal 1987, which ended in March 1988, turned out to be 5.2 percent. That for fiscal 1988 is estimated to be almost the same. This high growth was driven exclusively by domestic demand. The contribution of domestic demand to the real growth rate in fiscal 1987 was 6.7 percent; that of external demand was minus 1.4 percent. This very substantial reduction in external demand, reflected in Japan's shrinking current account surplus, has played and will continue to play a significant role in the expansion of the world economy. In this section, we will consider the deflationary impact of this revaluation and the mechanism of recovery.

Three deflationary forces
The 60 percent appreciation of the yen between the Plaza Accord of September 1985 and July 1986 had a deflationary impact on business conditions in Japan through three main routes, and thereby brought about a high-yen recession. The first was that the appreciation reduced export volume and increased import volume, thus leading to deterioration in the aggregate demand after January 1986, as is shown clearly in Figure 7. On a volume basis, this reduction of the surpluses was rather rapid.

The second route was the triggering effect that the developments in trade had on inventory adjustments. These adjustments came at both the merchandise and raw material levels. The former was generated by the excess buildup of merchandise inventories after the fall in export quantities, and excess inventories were drawn down through lowering of production. This lowering had a direct deflationary impact. In addition, the appreciation of the yen meant that the yen prices of imported goods fell and therefore that holders of imported raw materials suffered capital losses.

In order to avoid such losses, inventories of raw materials were compressed at both the raw material and distribution levels. Thus, at the manufacturing, distribution, and import levels, the yen appreciation was the starting point for a large-scale reduction of inventories.

The third route of deflationary impact from the higher yen was the worsening of corporate profits centering on export-related manufacturing industries due to sharp declines in export prices in yen terms. This worsening, together with the impact through the first route, brought a reduction of plant and equipment investment in the tradable goods sector along with effects on consumption resulting from reductions in employment.

Let us consider the relative influence of these deflationary routes by looking at their relationship to the growth rate in FY 1986 (April 1986 through March 1987). Table 6 shows the real growth rates for fiscal years 1984 through 1987 along with the contributions of each component of demand. The real growth rate for 1986 was, as shown in the table, a rather low 2.7 percent. Looking at the composition, however, one sees first of all that the largest negative contribution came from the foreign balance, which subtracted 0.9 percent from the growth rate. That is to say, domestic demand alone would have led to a 3.6 percent growth rate. Second, the downward adjustment of inventories lowered overall growth by 0.4 percentage points. Thus, together these factors subtracted 1.3 percentage points from the growth rate, meaning that without their influences real growth in FY 1986 would have reached 4.0 percent. If one also considers the third recessionary route of the investment and employment adjustments by export-related industries, then real growth in 1986 would have reached the same level as in 1984 and 1985, merely on the strength of domestic demand expansion, had there been no deflationary impact from the higher yen.

Table 6.   Real GNP and contribution of each item (percentages)

Item	Fiscal year (April-March)				First Half (April-Sept. annual rate)	Second Half (Oct.-March annual rate)
	1984	1985	1986	1987		
1. Domestic demand	3.9	3.7	3.6	6.7	6.3	10.0
(1) Private sector	3.7	4.0	2.8	5.5	5.7	8.4
Final consumption	1.5	1.6	1.9	2.2	2.7	3.0
Housing investment	0.0	0.1	0.5	1.2	1.2	2.1
Investment in machinery and equipment	1.8	2.2	0.8	1.9	1.7	2.8
Inventory	0.4	0.1	-0.4	0.1	0.1	0.4
(2) Public sector	0.2	-0.3	0.8	0.9	0.8	1.5
Final consumption	0.3	0.2	0.3	0.2	0.2	0.1
Capital formation	-0.2	-0.5	0.5	0.8	0.6	1.3
Inventory	0.1	0.0	0.0	-0.1	-0.2	0.0
2. Current account surplus	1.3	0.8	-0.9	-1.5	-1.8	-1.5
Exports of goods and services	2.7	0.4	-0.7	0.9	0.9	1.5
Imports	-1.4	0.4	-0.3	-2.4	-2.7	-3.0
3. Gross national expenditure	5.1	4.5	2.7	4.9	4.4	8.4

The effects of gold bullion imported to mint coins to commemorate the Emperor's 60th year of reign (which affected public expenditures and imports) have been adjusted for by the estimation of the Research and Statistics Department, the Bank of Japan.

Three reasons for the recovery

With the start of 1987 and particularly after the announcement in June of the real GNP growth rate for the first quarter of the year of 4.9 percent vis-à-vis the previous quarter, the outlook for business conditions shifted suddenly. At that time research institutes and economists who had been forecasting real growth for fiscal 1987 of about 2 percent began to raise their forecasts toward 3 percent, while the government forecast of 3.5 percent seemed for the first time in months to be achievable. As already noted, the actual growth rate was a very high 5.2 percent. Developments on the tax front also supported the view that the strengthening of the business cycle was very solid. This came in the form of an unexpected natural increase in fiscal revenue of ¥2.4 trillion, of which more than half, or ¥1.3 trillion, was due to increases in corporate taxes due to the unexpectedly strong recovery of corporate profits. As seen in Figure 1, real GNP was indeed rising very rapidly in the first quarter of 1987.

We must now ask why the Japanese economy confounded the majority of forecasters and conquered the high-yen recession so unexpectedly and quickly, and why the prospect of business recovery opened so widely and speedily. Basically, as argued earlier, in Chapter 1, the reason was the ability of Japanese corporations to recover equilibrium. Even if we restrict discussion to the bounce back from the trough of this recession, three important factors in this ability to recover equilibrium can be distinguished.

The Cyclical Aspect of the High-Yen Recession

As we noted above, the 60 percent appreciation of the yen in the period up to July 1986 was followed by a period of more than a year (to October 1987) in which the value of the yen fluctuated within a ten-yen range around a central value of about ¥150 per dollar; in general terms, therefore, the yen was approximately stable. The deflationary effect of this 60 percent increase had thus begun by July 1986, and thereafter the cyclical recession period based on this effect proceeded without any further impact. After a few months it was only natural that there would be a cyclical business recovery, once business firms had adjusted to these deflationary factors.

Let us take another look at the three deflationary routes mentioned previously. First was the volume effect on exports and imports. A look at the trade balance on a volume basis as shown in Figure 7 reveals a steady declining trend until recently. Also, in Table 6, negative contribution to real growth rate of the external sector in the second half of fiscal 1987 was still minus 1.5 percent, which is comparable to minus 0.9 percent in fiscal 1986. We cannot find any sign of shrinking deflationary impacts through the first route.

However, the impact through the second route—that is, the cyclical recovery of inventories—deserves attention. During 1986, production by manufacturing industries grew by less than shipments, thus leading to a deflationary effect on production. As a result, the high level of finished goods inventories caused by the first impact declined steadily, thus ending a complete cycle in finished goods inventories by the middle of 1987. In addition, the movement toward inventory compression at the distribution and raw materials levels was influenced by a halt in the fall of import prices after the July 1986 lull in yen appreciation. At times there were even increases of certain inventories of this type. These developments indicate the end of the inventory adjustment at these levels. With the completion of this inventory adjustment, a fiscal contribution to growth from inventories changed from minus 0.4 percent in 1986 to plus 0.1 percent in fiscal 1987 (Table 6) so that real GNP growth rate in fiscal 1987 increased by 0.5 percentage points, all other things being equal.

The deflationary impact through the third route, the role of corporate profits, also constituted a cyclical factor in the recovery. As seen in the large natural increase in fiscal revenue, even the income of manufacturing industries related to exports saw a halt in the reduction of profits in the second half of 1986. These sectors had seen a large decrease in corporate profits in the two business periods after the Plaza Accord, i.e., in the second half of fiscal 1985 and the first half of fiscal 1986. This was due not only to the decline in export volume but also to the decline in yen prices of exports, since firms did not raise their foreign currency export prices to correspond to the full increase in the value of the yen. However, with the lull in the appreciation of the yen in the second half of fiscal 1986, the decline in yen-denominated export prices also ceased and began to rise, thus catching up with the increased yen value. As a result, the deterioration of cash flow ceased, and the fall in profits ceased as well. In future, to the extent that the yen remains stable, an increase in profits is likely, so that the investment and employment effects from this sector, which had been holding down growth, will also ease.

Thus, two of the three deflationary effects of the high yen have eased, and a lull in appreciation and in cyclical factors bringing about an improvement of the business cycle have come to the fore.

Merits of a strong yen and structural adjustment

A second factor that eased the recovery of equilibrium for corporations was the advent of beneficial effects from the strong yen. The large nominal appreciation of the yen after the Plaza Accord, as shown in Figure 6, resulted in a large appreciation in real terms. This implies a substantial improvement in Japan's terms of trade, that is, an increase in the quantities of foreign goods and services received for a given amount of Japanese goods and services provided.

Therefore, with a given amount of income or assets in the Japanese economy in yen terms, the quantity of foreign goods or services that can be purchased with that income or those assets has risen, so that there has been a corresponding increase in their real value. For example, individuals can buy more consumer goods with a given level of income, no matter whether they are buying at home or abroad. For corporations, the decline in the cost of imported raw materials and of foreign operations leads to an increase in corporate profits. In addition, proceeds of sales of domestic assets can buy more foreign assets.

When the increase in purchasing power for individuals and corporations is realized in demand, then business conditions in Japan are naturally stimulated. In fact, as shown clearly in Table 6, private consumption and residential investment have been contributing very large amounts to growth (a combined contribution of 3.8 percentage points in fiscal 1987). Although these developments were also influenced by the policy actions described below, they were to some extent an expression of the benefits of the strong yen in the household sector.

The benefits of the strong yen in the corporate sector have been expressed in increases in domestic investment and employment along with increases in direct investment abroad (e.g., the building of factories in foreign countries). In 1986 and 1987, both plant and equipment investment and employment fell in the manufacturing sector, because of the deflationary impact of the rising yen on exports. However, investment and employment have increased in nonmanufacturing, which is enjoying the advantages of yen appreciation, so that an overall steady increase in these indicators has been maintained.

Yen appreciation has also stimulated a reorientation of Japanese industry. The proportion of industries that rely on expanding exports, and hindering imports, and that have been hurt by the impact of deflationary effects from the high yen is on the decline; there is a rising proportion of industries that encourage imports, serve domestic demand, and enjoy the benefits of the strong yen. In this process of reorientation, one constantly hears of the adjustment of investment and employment in the former sector as a negative factor in business conditions. This view, however, is one-sided. Whenever certain industries are declining, others are developing, and these developing industries (for example, information, telecommunications, or finance) have enjoyed the advantages of the high yen and are experiencing expansion of investment and employment. These latter movements are major supports to the current growth of the Japanese economy.

Effects of fiscal and monetary policies
A third factor helping firms to recover equilibrium has been the effects of fiscal and monetary policies. Let us consider them in turn, looking first at monetary policy. The discount rate was lowered to 2.5 percent by February 1987, and various interest rates since then have remained at historically low levels. As a result, the rate of increase in the money supply (defined on an M2 + CD basis) had reached 12 percent on a year-on-year basis toward the end of 1987. This indicates a condition of extreme ease on a quantitative basis. There is no doubt that these low interest rates and the quantitative ease in monetary policy have helped to support residential investment and plant and equipment investment.

Moreover, easy monetary policy has raised the price of existing assets such as land, golf club memberships, stocks, and bonds. As a result, wealth effects have raised consumption and stimulated residential and plant and equipment investment. To give a concrete example, individuals have seen the value of their assets rise through price increases of land and stocks, and as a result have decreased their savings and increased their consumption, as well as selling some assets and increasing investment. In the case of corporations, assets have been sold and thus contributed to nonoperating profits, while assets that were retained have been used as collateral for borrowings to support new investments.

These wealth effects are part of a process that occurs whenever monetary easing attempts to stimulate business recovery. At the bottoms of business cycles, when expected profit rates are low, funds that are in abundant supply flow to existing assets that have a tendency for price increases over the long run. However, as a result of these flows, the prices of such existing assets will be bid up, so that high rates of appreciation can no longer be expected. On the contrary, the business cycle itself will be stimulated by wealth effects. As the expected rate of profit on investments thus increases, funds will turn from existing assets to new plant and equipment investment and inventory investment. The period of the rise of prices of existing assets is a period of transition until a new investment phase begins.

Although a period of increase in existing asset prices is part of the path to equilibrium and recovery, these price increases have certain undesirable side effects. First is the unfair redistribution of income due to increases in the value of land and housing, which make it more difficult for younger age groups to acquire home ownership. A second such adverse effect is that the higher prices of stocks and bonds in the markets will inevitably be followed by price decreases when monetary conditions tighten, with the result that sizable losses will be sustained by financial institutions holding these assets in large quantities.

In order to counteract the first of these adverse effects, several types of policies are necessary, including such thoroughgoing land-use policies as deregulation, tax reform,

and extension of commuting infrastructure, along with redevelopment of urban centers. If such policies can contain
the tendency for land prices to rise over the long run, then
funds will cease to flow into investments in land during
periods of financial ease. In fact, the chief villains in the rise
of land prices have been land-use policy and the absence
of urban redevelopment; financial ease has only been an
accomplice.

The second adverse effect is largely an issue of the avoidance of capital loss through proper risk management of
assets and liabilities by financial institutions; this is their
own responsibility. However, when easy monetary conditions continue for too long, a larger portion of assets will
face the possibility of large decreases in price, with the
potential to injure the soundness of the system as a whole.

The reasons for high stock prices

Understanding the reason stock prices in Japan are high will
help us to understand the structural aspects of the economy.

In the first half of the 1980s, the average price earnings
ratio (PER) of Japanese corporate stocks was already around
20 to 25, about twice as high as in other countries. In 1986
the PER started to rise further, and is now around 60, while
those in other countries have remained stable between 10
and 15.

While there are various ways to explain this extremely
high PER, we focus on two representative ones: the *flow
approach*, which draws on economic fundamentals to explain
the high PER; and the *stock approach*, which can explain
the rapid rise since 1986.

The flow approach explains the high PER by considering
such factors as the high growth rate of corporate profits
(the highest rate among member countries) and the low
level of interest rates (the lowest). In addition to these economic factors, institutional factors are involved. Japanese

corporations tend to hold each other's shares. This mutual stock sharing among major corporations, which in some cases amounts to more than half of a company's stock, leads to high PERs by reducing the number of shares available for purchase on the market by non-corporate buyers. The prices of such available shares naturally rise, and so does the PER.

Another factor that must be kept in mind is the difference in accounting practices between Japan and the United States in the reporting of corporate profits: straight line depreciation is generally adopted in the U.S., while exponential depreciation is often used in Japan. This difference results in lower reported profits for Japanese corporations.

Although the flow approach explains the high PERs already recorded in the first half of the 1980s, it fails to explain the recent dramatic upsurge. More useful in this sense is the stock approach, sometimes also called the "Tobin's q approach," which emphasizes the importance of the market value of assets held by corporations. In these terms, for example, the implicit market value of stock in major corporations has been increased by the rapid rise in Tokyo land prices in the latter half of the 1980s, which resulted in unrealized capital gains for corporate landowners.

It is probable that share prices will turn downward once interest rates start going up, as they are expected to do, since low interest rates are one of the primary reasons for high PERs. However, I do not expect a repeat of the disastrous situation we saw at the time of the October 1987 market crash. Japanese stock prices have remained high for institutional reasons, as well as economic ones.

Fiscal policies

Let us next consider the effects of fiscal policies. After the early implementation of fiscal expenditure in FY 1986, a supplementary budget of ¥3 trillion was introduced. This supplementary budget was at first criticized as having very little in actual new expenditures, but on closer examination it was clear that, at least in terms of GNP accounting, fiscal expenditure would contribute by 0.8 percentage points to growth in fiscal 1986. This positive contribution was the first in several years. As shown in Table 6, fiscal expenditure had for some time contributed almost nothing to growth because of fiscal consolidation efforts, but this changed in fiscal 1986.

In fiscal 1987, front-loaded expenditure in public construction was implemented, followed by a supplementary budget of ¥6 trillion. The result was a contribution of 0.9 percentage points to real GNP growth rate from public-sector expenditure in fiscal 1987, as confirmed by the data in Table 6.

To summarize: the strong recovery of Japanese domestic demand in 1987 was mainly attributable to three reasons. The first was the diminution of the extremely sharp deflationary impact of the 60 percent appreciation of the yen, from 240 yen per dollar to 150 yen, over a ten-month period from immediately after the Plaza Accord in September 1985 to July 1986. The rate of the appreciation of the yen after July 1986 was much more gradual, which permitted business firms to adapt more smoothly to the new circumstances.

The second reason for the strong recovery of domestic demand was the effect of the improvement in Japan's terms of trade caused by the tremendous appreciation of the yen. On the demand side, the prices of final goods and services declined a great deal, due to the decrease in the price of imported goods, and this resulted in an increase in real income, which in turn caused a strong expansion in private consumption and in residential construction. On the supply side, the improvement in the terms of trade was reflected in a decline in the costs to business firms for imported raw

materials and energy. The supply side of the Japanese economy has benefited so much through this reduction in costs
that the resultant increase in profitability ignited a recovery
in plant and equipment investment.

The third reason for the strong recovery was that macroeconomic policy was extremely effective. Monetary policy
had expansionary effects upon the economy through three
channels. The first channel was interest rates, which in
1988 were at their lowest levels in history. Second, as the
money growth rate of 12 percent in terms of M2 + CDs
demonstrates, financial conditions in the private sector are
accommodative enough to support rapid expansion of private demand. The third transmission channel was through
the wealth effect. Prices of assets such as land, equities, and
bonds have risen remarkably due to easy monetary conditions. On the fiscal policy side, the front-loaded expenditure
of public construction was implemented in 1987, followed
by a supplementary budget of ¥6 trillion.

For these three reasons, the Japanese economy turned
back again to the equilibrium growth path described in
Chapter 1.

Revival of Sustainable Growth on an Equilibrium Path

The domestic demand-led growth of the Japanese economy,
initiated by the three factors discussed above, continued
through the course of fiscal 1988, although its driving forces
changed. In 1987, the triggers for the strong recovery were
exogenous stimuli, including the expansionary effects of
macroeconomic policies and improvement in the terms of
trade. The Japanese economy, set in motion by these exogenous factors, will continue to expand spontaneously
through an endogenous virtuous circle within the private
sector. One can compare the economy to the engine of a

car—once the starter has turned over, the engine continues to run without any further help from the starter. The fundamental reason for this self-sustained economic growth was discussed in Chapter 1. Here, I will describe it from the point of view of actual developments in GNP components in 1988.

Spontaneous increase in private expenditure

How will this virtuous circle operate within the market economy? To begin with investment in plant and equipment, in 1987 such investment was concentrated largely in the nontradable goods sector, thanks to the improvement in the terms of trade caused by the tremendous appreciation of the yen. But in 1988, in addition to a continuing increase in investment in the nontradable goods sector, investment in the tradable goods sector, centering on the manufacturing industry, also picked up. This recovery in investment was not export-oriented, but was rather induced by the strong expansion of domestic demand. Foreign demand for Japanese products is now being met through Japanese direct investment in production facilities overseas, and products from these plants have started to be imported back to Japan, such as Honda cars from the United States.

Real private consumption increased more rapidly in 1987 than the increase in the nominal wage rate negotiated during the spring labor offensive, which was only a 3.5 percent rise, because the consumer price index remained constant owing to the improvement in the terms of trade and recovered employment. But in 1988, the situation was different. The nominal spring wage rise was higher than that of the previous year by 1 percentage point, and summer bonuses increased by 5.5 percent over the year. Both were certainly a reflection of the improvement in business profits. In addition, employment was increasing at a faster pace. The continuous expansion of private consumption in 1988 was a natural phenomenon in the course of a trade cycle, and was independent of any further exogenous stimuli such as an improvement in the terms of trade and expansionary policies. Although residential construction was leveling off, the share of residential construction in GNP was only 6 percent while the combined share of fixed investment and private consumption in real GNP was 75 percent. Since the two main components of GNP, fixed investment and private consumption, will increase steadily, expansion of private domestic demand in 1988 and toward the next year was not expected to weaken; hence the fiscal policy stance should no longer be stimulative, but rather be neutral in 1988 and 1989.

This is typical sustained growth in the classical model of economics described in Chapter 1. Expansion in production and fixed investment on the profit maximization path of the business sector stimulates expansion in private sector consumption through increased employment and higher wages, which in turn stimulate further expansion in production and fixed investment in the business sector.

Sustainability of equilibrium growth

The remaining issue is how long this domestic demand-led growth and the decreasing trend in the current account surplus will continue. Sustainability depends on three aspects of the economy. The first is the demand side of the economy. The current virtuous circle in private demand—that is, from production to employment, employment to private consumption, and then private consumption to further production and fixed investment—will continue in 1989 and into the 1990s, if the other two aspects, external shocks and supply considerations, do not jeopardize the economy.

The Japanese economy since the end of World War II has never faced a recession caused by spontaneous weakening of domestic demand. Until the middle of the 1960s, a boom was always ended by tight monetary and fiscal policy to cope with balance of payment deficits under the Bretton Woods system of the pegged exchange rate. In 1970 and 1973, when balance of payment was still in surplus, recessions began owing to contractionary monetary and fiscal policy to fight inflation caused by the shortage of supply capacity. In these pre-1973 experiences, economic growth could not be sustained because the supply side of the economy including the ability to import could not keep up with the strong demand.

Since the shift to the floating exchange rate system as well as to the low growth period by Japanese standards, booms occurred in 1979–1980 and 1984–1985, both attributable to increases in net exports with the weak yen. They naturally came to an end, when net exports stopped expanding as the second oil crisis caused a worldwide recession after 1981 and as the yen appreciated after September 1985 under the Plaza Accord. These experiences clearly show that without external shocks and the supply side shortage, Japanese economic growth is likely to be sustained.

In the near future, even if the growth in private demand slows down, fiscal policy can become expansionary again, precisely because in 1988 it was neutral. In fact, the government plans a large-scale tax cut as part of the process of tax reform in 1989. Also, if necessary, a policy of front-loading public expenditure followed by a supplementary budget can be implemented again. As far as the demand side of the economy is concerned, the sustainability of the present domestic demand-led growth in the next few years is well assured.

The second point to be discussed concerns external shocks. If the U.S. budget deficit is cut substantially from fiscal 1990, as is likely, the resulting slowdown in the U.S. economy will influence demand in Japan. However, considering that the present economic growth of Japan has been and will continue to be led by domestic demand with external demand contributing negatively to economic growth, such a demand shock from abroad will not seriously threaten the sustainability of Japanese economic growth. A substantial cut in the U.S. budget deficit is a necessary measure for the world economy in any case.

The second type of possible external shock is a further appreciation of the yen. But currently the yen seems stable against the dollar and major European currencies. There are a number of reasons that account for this stability of exchange rates. First of all, international imbalances have been narrowing; second, policy coordination in support of the stability of exchange rates has been successful since the Louvre Accord. It is quite unlikely that the dollar will undergo a further large fall. Even if the yen appreciates, as long as it does so gradually the Japanese economy will not be buffeted very much, as experience in 1987 and 1988 indicates. Indeed, the Japanese economy has demonstrated a remarkable ability to adjust itself positively to such circumstances.

The third type of external shock is a financial shock from abroad. But as the events of October 1987 show, the central banks of major countries are well able to stabilize their financial systems, and, further, international policy coordination to sustain the global financial system has now been well established. While we should not be too optimistic or complacent, I do not think that one should be too pessimistic, either. The fourth type of external shock to the Japanese economy would be a hefty increase in oil prices. This possibility is not likely although oil prices might rise slowly near the end of this century. In general, the Japanese economy is unlikely to be seriously affected by external shocks.

The third point concerns the supply side of the Japanese economy. If the supply side cannot accommodate the rapid expansion of domestic demand, then bottlenecks may appear in some sectors. Also, if international commodity prices continue to rise under the stable yen rate, the inflationary trends in international markets will be eventually reflected in the price trends in the Japanese domestic market. This kind of imported inflation, together with the possibility of domestic bottlenecks, are the main concerns vis-à-vis the supply side of the Japanese economy. If the above scenario actually takes place, then with the low velocity of money caused by the high monetary growth rate of 10 to 12 percent in 1987 and 1988, speculative inventory investments could easily be made on a large scale. Vigilance concerning the recent trend in high money growth is thus warranted.

To summarize: the domestic demand-led growth that is accompanied by a steady decrease in the current account surplus can be sustained if Japan succeeds in maintaining domestic price stability.

Decrease in current account surplus and associated structural changes
Finally, it should be stressed that the decreasing trend in the current account surplus is firmly established because it is based on structural changes in the economy. As the negative contribution of external demand to the real growth rate implies, the decreasing trend in the current account surplus in real terms has been steady, and the ratio of the current account surplus to GNP, which once reached 4.5 percent in fiscal 1986, declined to 3.3 percent in fiscal 1987, and is estimated to decline to nearly 2.5 percent in fiscal 1988.

One of the striking features behind this trend is the fact that Japan for the first time in its history has reached the stage at which horizontal trade with neighboring Asian countries has become possible. Neighboring Asian countries, particularly the newly industrializing economies (NIEs), have reached a level of industrialization where they can export finished manufacturing goods to Japan. At the same time, because of the tremendous appreciation of the yen, Japan must focus its exports on high value-added finished goods and its imports on low value-added finished goods from neighboring Asian countries. The ratio of finished goods in Japan's imports, which historically was 10 to 20 percent, exceeded 50 percent in September 1988.

Policy Issues for the Future

Thus, the Japanese economy overcame the shock of a 60 percent appreciation of the yen in 1987 and turned back to a sustainable growth path in 1987–88. The outlook for the future, however, involves many issues, not only in macroeconomic policy but also in policies for structural adjustment.

Issues in macroeconomic policy

Concerning the content of macroeconomic policy, monetary policy has continued in a state of extreme ease since early 1986 while fiscal policy implemented early public investment expenditures in May of 1987 and a ¥6 trillion stimulus package in July, centering on increases in public investment and income tax cuts. This macroeconomic policy has provided more than enough stimulus. Real growth in the first three quarters of 1988 over the same period of the previous year was as high as 6.8 percent.

Exchange rate movements, however, suggest an element of uncertainty. If the current account surplus were to rise again, appreciation of the yen would begin again as well. This is particularly worrisome because it is unlikely, as mentioned above, that the United States will begin a serious fiscal expenditure-cutting effort until fiscal 1990 or make enough efforts to reduce the trade deficit through domestic demand suppression.

Because of such factors a recurrence of yen appreciation and dollar weakening could occur after a re-expansion of the deficit surplus relationship between the United States and Japan. Still, abstracting from the possibility of a collapse of the dollar, any appreciation of the yen is likely to be in the range of about ¥10. One cannot of course deny the possibility of temporary shocks. Nevertheless, such an appreciation would amount on average to no more than 8 percent. The deflationary impact from such an event would therefore not be large, and the possibility that the Japanese economy would therefore fall into a recession appears minor. In fact, some of the effect of a somewhat stronger yen might be desirable in order to sustain growth, as this might aid price stability in the face of more than sufficiently expansionary macro policies and changes in the industrial structure.

The real issue is the possibility of inflation from sectors related to domestic demand, as discussed above. The benefits of a stronger yen and stimulative macroeconomic policies have already increased the likelihood that the growth of domestic demand in fiscal 1988 will, just as in the previous year, lead to overall economic growth of more than 5 percent. Therefore, there is a possibility that bottlenecks may emerge in some sectors and generate increases in prices and wages. If such pressures develop, it would be beneficial if total supply were expanded through additions to imports.

In a situation with a strong yen, price increases that come from domestic demand would be eliminated by imports. But this argument can be countered: in the international markets for commodities, the period of disinflation in the first half of the 1980s has ended, and a tendency has emerged for prices to increase for many commodities, e.g., petrochemicals, nonferrous metals, and lumber. One may well conclude that stability in the domestic markets for such commodities due to the strong yen may be only temporary.

Another factor is the potential for homemade inflation: even if the imported costs of raw materials fall due to the strengthening of the yen, the sum of unit profits and wages per unit of production (that is, the GNP deflator) might rise, accompanying the emergence of bottlenecks. In such circumstances there would be an outbreak of homemade inflation.

Macroeconomic policy therefore must adopt an attitude of sufficient caution with respect to the outbreak of inflation. Public works investment must be implemented so as not to engender bottlenecks through such factors as a shortage of skilled workers, order queues for particular materials, or regional overconcentration. From the viewpoint of avoiding bottlenecks and aiming at a smaller government, expansionary fiscal policy should therefore place more weight on tools such as income and corporate tax cuts.

In monetary policy, the extreme financial ease brought about by the discount rate cut of February 1987 should be reversed if necessary. In order to return to a normal period of monetary ease and to extend the recovery of business conditions that has now begun, it is absolutely necessary to take such precautionary measures. On the quantitative side, the growth rate of M2+CDs, which reached 12 percent in the first quarter of 1988 on a year-on-year basis, should be gradually reduced to 8–9 percent, and to this end the extraordinarily low interest rates should be gradually corrected. Nevertheless, sharp changes in monetary growth rates that would lead to sharp interest rate increases should be avoided because of the potential effect of needless shocks to the economy in the form of sudden changes in stock, bond, and other markets, as well as in the foreign exchange market. If the 12 percent increases in the money supply were to continue, so that the two-year moving average rate of money increase also came to 12 percent, then there would be a high probability of an outbreak of homemade inflation. That is, if one views as desirable a GNP deflator inflation rate of about 1.0 percent with real growth of 5.0 percent, then the corresponding rate of increase of M2 + CDs must not exceed 8–9 percent, even if one keeps in mind the reduction of monetary velocity for such reasons as interest rate liberalization. Fortunately, that money growth rate had declined to 10 percent by the end of 1988.

Higher per capita income than the United States

In considering the future of the Japanese economy, structural adjustment is as important a topic as sustainable growth without inflation. In 1987, the exchange rate averaged ¥143.86 per dollar, and per capita GNP in Japan, which was ¥19,650 at this average rate, exceeded that of the United States, which was ¥18,558. But Japanese who know the United States and its standard of living feel that such a calculation is completely misleading. Why then should such a statistic be derived?

If a purchasing power parity exchange rate for the yen were calculated with the consumer price index, which is most closely related to daily life, then a rate of more than ¥200 per dollar would be calculated. Some people therefore think that the recent rates of ¥130 per dollar are therefore excessively strong. However, as can be understood by looking at Figure 6, purchasing power parity rates of about ¥130 per dollar would be calculated using the wholesale price index for manufactured goods. Therefore the exchange rate of ¥143 per dollar is not so much stronger than the purchasing power parity rate in the 1970s.

The reason why this calculation does not ring true stems from the following aspects of the structure of prices in Japan. As elsewhere, the prices of goods and services that are purchased by consumers in Japan are those of both tradable goods and nontradable goods; while the former have a purchasing power parity exchange rate of ¥130 per dollar, the latter have a rate exceeding ¥200 per dollar. Therefore, per capita GNP in Japan would exceed that of the United

States if the former rate were used for the conversion, even though this calculation would not make any sense to an average Japanese who compares the standards of living in the two countries through direct experience that includes the latter purchasing power parity rate.

In Japan, these nontradable goods are extraordinarily expensive. An extreme example of this is the price of land (also reflected in the level of rents). Moreover, a large number of agricultural products that ought to be tradable goods have in fact become nontradables and are therefore expensive. This means that two of the three daily necessities of life (food, clothing, and shelter) are either several times or tens of times more expensive in Japan than elsewhere, and this fact is not reflected in the exchange rate. This is why the per capita GNP calculation at an exchange rate of ¥130 per dollar does not seem to make sense. Such a price structure implies extreme inefficiencies in resource allocation. Without decisive agricultural and land-use policies to reduce food and land prices, people will never feel that Japanese GNP per capita has exceeded that of the United States.

Land-use policy is basically an issue of policy for the Tokyo metropolitan area. Technological advances will be important in improving land utilization. For example, advances in the technology of superconductivity have recently made the application of linear motor technology to railways a likelihood in the near future. The crucial policies in improving land use will therefore be to spread the residential areas of Tokyo and shift business and government functions that have concentrated in the city to outlying areas, as sharp reductions in commuting times become feasible. This might be accomplished by the construction of a network of commuter lines, the promotion of emigration from Tokyo by raising the tax on assets holdings in the city, lowering of the capital gains tax on incomes from property sales, and the relaxation of regulations inhibiting construction.

The central points for agricultural policy changes would lie in a steady deregulation of agricultural markets and a gradual cut in price supports along with the abolition of various types of regulations that have prevented large-scale farm management and rational farm operations. Typical commodities that would be involved in liberalizing the agricultural markets are rice, beef, and oranges.

Both of these structural adjustment policies have difficult political aspects. However, if Japan does not succeed in structural adjustment in these two areas, there will be major constraints on the further development of the economy.

Finally, tax reform should be mentioned. When the tax reform bill of fiscal 1987 was presented in the Diet in January 1987, the following column of mine appeared in *Nihon Keizai Shimbun* under the title "Support Tax Reform":

The outlines of tax reform have now been solidified and will shortly be presented to the Diet. The Liberal Democratic Party and Ministry of Finance are currently busy in creating a consensus for the bill, and the opposition forces are now sharpening their tactics.

To put the conclusion first, we advocate strongly the adoption of this tax reform. This is not because the bill as it stands has no disadvantages. In fact, the disadvantages are not few. But a frustration of tax reform at this point would mean the continuation of the even worse tax system that currently prevails. The flaws can be corrected after the reform is implemented.

The worst aspects of the current tax system are that it skews tax burdens toward wage earners from whom it is easy to collect taxes and toward profitable corporations, that it is extremely unfair, and that it distorts market mechanisms at the same time. Attempts to rectify the taxation of firms that pretend to be unprofitable and individual proprietorships that currently escape taxation would involve extremely high administrative costs and social costs and therefore generate inefficiencies.

The reformed tax law would lower taxation on "honest" wage-income earners and profitable corporations, with a corresponding shift of taxation to the so-called "dishonest." This could be done because the income that is concealed from the tax authorities must be either spent or invested in financial assets, and so the new sales tax on expenditure and the across-the-board withholding tax on interest income on financial assets, to the extent these assets earn interest, would level out the tax burden. Moreover, the administrative and social costs of this new tax system would not necessarily be high. In addition, because the new tax rates are flatter, the new tax system would be relatively neutral with respect to the market mechanism.

There are many questions here for debate. Among these are whether the income tax tables maintain vertical fairness, whether a fair withholding tax on the capital gains on securities and other tax-avoiding financial products should be levied, whether the extent of exclusions from the sales tax has been determined fairly, and a large number of other topics.

The branches of this tree of tax reform may be cut, pared, and directed later, but the work of planting the tree itself must be undertaken now while the chance is available. Otherwise this chance may be lost for some time.

Unfortunately, the tax reform itself ran into difficulties because the government's approach to the sales tax was poor and because there was a weak sense of connection between the tax cut and the tax reform aspects of the bill.

As a result, only the income tax cut and the elimination of tax preferences on savings were enacted by the Diet. In order to call forth work from the Japanese people and to support corporate activity in times of difficulty, a large-scale cut of income and corporate tax is necessary. It is desirable from the viewpoints of fairness, efficiency, and neutrality to finance such cuts with the introduction of a broad-based, low-rate, simple indirect tax. It is also best to correct the balance between direct and indirect taxes and to simplify the tax system.

Such a tax cut has been enacted by the Diet in the form of a consumption tax, a type of value-added tax, which takes effect in fiscal 1989. The task remaining for the future is keeping the consumption tax rate low to prevent the government from growing in size.

Even after the success of the tax reform proposals, there will still be two major issues to deal with. One will be a thoroughgoing reform of the land tax system. The second will be the international standardization of the tax system. As financial globalization proceeds, retention of tax systems that are unique to Japan will only strengthen international friction from the demands for a level playing field, or else result in a hollowing out of the Japanese tax base through Japan's defeat in the international competition among systems.

Part II

Japan's Role in the World Economy

The first two chapters of this book considered what has occurred in the Japanese economy since the move to floating exchange rates. In the course of that analysis many problems were identified, including a number that will become major issues in the future. Among them, two are perhaps of greatest importance. One is the possibility of a worldwide depression, triggered by turmoil in the foreign exchange and financial markets. What could Japan's role be in preventing such an occurrence?

The other is the outlook for the international monetary system. The system of the future will be based on two changes: Japan's replacing the United States as the world's major creditor country, and the simultaneous globalization of the financial system. What will Japan's role be in this new world monetary regime?

These issues will be considered in the following three chapters. Chapter 3 discusses the possibility of a depression, Chapter 4 the international monetary system, and Chapter 5 Japan's ongoing financial reform in response to international needs.

91

3

Can a World Depression Recur?

With the collapse of the stock market boom in the United States in October 1929, there occurred a worldwide depression that lasted until 1933. This depression involved a withering of real economic activity on a worldwide scale, credit panics, and default on liabilities by exporters of primary commodities. Today, there are people who wonder about the possibility of the recurrence of such a worldwide depression. Different people have put forth different possible scenarios for such an occurrence, but an element common to them all is a collapse of the dollar leading to worldwide recession and credit panic. Some had premonitions of this nightmare scenario on October 19, 1987, when a crash of stock prices occurred in the New York market, followed by a sizable drop in the dollar's value.

A Scenario of World Depression

The first element in a depression scenario is the failure of further budget consolidation in the United States, due to factors such as continuing confrontation between Republi-

93

can and Democratic policymakers or a failure of U.S.–
Soviet arms reduction negotiations. In these circumstances,
reduction in the current account deficit in the United States
would come to a halt, and that deficit would instead begin
to show signs of increasing, just as signs of inflation in the
U.S. domestic economy strengthened. As a result, confidence in the U.S. economy and economic policy, and therefore in the dollar, would be lost, and the dollar would collapse, creating reluctance on the part of foreign investors
to invest in the United States, sales of dollar-denominated
assets already held (capital flight), or a rush to sell dollars
in the forward market (hedging) that would bring a collapse
of the spot dollar.

Due to cost-push pressures from the effect of the falling
dollar on import prices in the United States and to the
arbitrage effects on dollar-denominated prices of raw materials in world markets, a worldwide inflation would begin.
At the same time, long-term interest rates in the United
States would surge as capital inflows were reduced and as
a reflection of higher expected interest rates. For policy
reasons as well, such as defending the dollar and suppressing
inflation, the governors of the Federal Reserve would raise
interest rates. As a result, a business downturn would begin
and a simultaneous inflation and recession would occur;
that is to say, the world would fall into stagflation.

Japan and the Federal Republic of Germany (and the
EMS countries that are centered on the Deutsche-mark)
would at the same time fall into a recession due to the effects
on exports of the double foreign shock of strong currencies
and the recession in the United States. Therefore, a simultaneous recession would occur in the United States, Japan,
and Europe. As a result, the indebted countries, especially
those in Latin America, would see exports stagnate just as
the interest payments they make on their dollar-denominated debts rise with the increase in world interest rates.

Their economic recovery plans would be hit from both sides. There would then be defaults on both interest and principal repayments of their debts to banks.

After these events, banks in the United States would face a shortage of liquidity due to tight monetary policy, and bankruptcies would increase as a result of default on interest and principal repayments from debtor countries along with a deterioration of the quality of domestic assets due to the domestic recession. Because of the globalization of finance through electronic networks in the world financial system, a financial panic in the United States would, because of the central position of New York as one of the key elements in this world financial system, cause domino-like reactions throughout the world, and a worldwide financial panic could not but occur.

This is the broad outline of the scenario according to those who foresee another world depression.

Superficial similarities

One of the background elements in such scenarios is a number of superficial similarities between 1929 and the present. Because of these similarities, one naturally compares the experiences of those times with the present using the outlook of today.

The first similarity is a change in the world's largest creditor nation. In the 1920s, just after the First World War, the United Kingdom, which had been the key-currency nation under the international gold standard until that time, had passed its prime, and its trade deficit was beginning to expand. Because, however, of the income on past foreign investments, the nontrade accounts were in substantial surplus, so that the current account balance did not fall into deficit. However, the surplus began to decline, and as a result investment outflows to primary-product-producing countries began to thin.

In place of the United Kingdom, the United States began to increase its economic power. The United States had a continuous trade surplus during that era and its capital exports were expanding. The change of places between the United States and the United Kingdom in both international trade and capital outflows at that time corresponds to the relationship of the United States and Japan today.

A second major similarity concerns currency movements. The return to the gold standard at the old parity by the United Kingdom in April 1925 was the turning point for the worsening of the British trade balance and the emergence of a chronic surplus in the U.S. trade balance. Because the economic power of the United Kingdom had been relatively weakened, the pound was clearly overvalued at its old parity, although in fact the pound was considerably stronger than at any time since 1920. The United Kingdom maintained this exchange rate for the pound until September 1931, when the gold standard was suspended. As a result of those exchange rate movements, there were six years in which the United Kingdom was disadvantaged relative to the United States in terms of price competitiveness. A corresponding set of circumstances now is observed in the large current account deficit of the United States and the large current account surplus of Japan, resulting from the strength of the dollar in the first half of the 1980s.

Because the strength of the pound from 1925 through 1931 occurred under the gold standard system and the strength of the dollar between 1982 and 1985 under the floating exchange rate system, the reasons for these overvaluations were different: the former was the result of an unreasonable attempt to return to the gold standard while the latter was the result of a mix of policies. Nevertheless, the high value of the pound in terms of purchasing power parity vis-à-vis the dollar did continue for five years and was decisive in the change in the world's largest debtor country. On this point, history was indeed similar to what has happened more recently.

A third point of similarity was the extreme lengths to which the money game was taken by corporations and high-income individuals as symbolized by the stock market booms in the United States in 1927 through 1929. The stock market crash of October 1929 was the beginning of the world depression, and this seems precisely like a recurrence of the extreme lengths to which the money game in Japan is being taken today.

A fourth similarity is the existence of highly indebted countries. The high-debt countries of today are the oil producing countries of Latin America (Argentina, Mexico, Venezuela, etc.), while at the time of the world depression of 1929, the debtor countries were also Latin American but agricultural countries (Bolivia, Peru, Chile, Brazil, Costa Rica, etc.). Just as the decline of oil prices in 1986 worsened the indebtedness problems of today, a collapse of agricultural prices due to overproduction worsened the indebtedness problems of the primary producing countries of 1929. Until that time the United Kingdom had supported the agricultural countries with a stable flow of capital, but then its economic power gradually weakened. When the United States replaced the United Kingdom the former had no interest in development investments, but rather concentrated on high-earning portfolio investments. As a result, there was a reduction of investment in the primary-product-producing countries that were suffering from low agricultural prices.

Today as well, the United States is losing its power to send capital to the countries of Latin America and to continue its economic assistance. Japan, which has now replaced the United States, is also concentrating on high-earning securities investments for its capital outflows so that, like the United States in the earlier period, capital exports are unstable.

The Historical Pattern of the Great Depression

If one looks only at these four superficial similarities, one may well be surprised. However, these four points composed only one of many aspects of the world depression of that time, and in some rather important ways the economic conditions of today are quite different.

When considering the scenario that led to the world depression of 1929, it is necessary to separate the process into at least three periods. The first is the period of the 1920s before the great crash in the United States in October 1929. The second is the period from the great crash until September 1931, at which time the United Kingdom suspended the gold standard. This period was a relatively standard recession for the times in question. The third period is that from September 1931 until April 1933, when the United States suspended the gold standard. During this period the collapse of the pound and the tight money policy in the United States worsened the economic conditions and brought about widespread financial panics.

The scenarios noted above for a repetition of the great depression through the collapse of the dollar are similar to the third period, in which there was a collapse of the pound. However, these scenarios seem to have a tendency to lump the various similarities together conveniently without distinguishing sufficiently between the three periods. These three periods are considered separately below.

Before October 1929

Despite the exhaustion of the United Kingdom during the First World War (1914–1918) through the relative loss of international competitiveness, an accumulation of fiscal deficits, and indebtedness to the United States, the United Kingdom returned to the gold standard at the prewar parity in April 1925. This point was the beginning of the precrash period. As noted above, artificial overvaluation of the pound posed continuous problems for the United Kingdom because of the pound crisis and also caused a change in the world's largest creditor nation from the United Kingdom to the United States. In the United States there was a steady expansion of economic growth over the medium term even though there were periodic fluctuations of the business cycle such as the two-year upswing from 1921 and the one-year downswing thereafter, the former being supported by a consumer demand boom in such durables as automobiles. After 1925, however, an export boom was added on top of this upswing due to the strength of the pound. As part of this long upswing, there was an increase in the degree of concentration of business in large corporations, which led to a shift of income toward such corporations and therefore to a shift in the distribution of income toward high-earning persons through high dividends and high stock prices. Consequences of this redistribution of income included an increase in the self-financing abilities of large corporations because of retained profits and an increase in the domestic savings rate based on the inherently high savings rates of high-income individuals. The result of this was a so-called money game, such as is also seen today. In the end, there was a boom in the domestic stock market and an increase in capital outflows focusing on securities investments.

This phenomenon had, as seen above, certain similarities to Japan today, but one must also recall the differences in the causes. Of course, the strength of the dollar in the first half of the 1980s, the excess savings of the United States at that time, and the excess savings of Japan today certainly bear a similarity to the earlier period, but this is the only similarity. In the United States during the great depression, the expansion of domestic activity and the increase in the income share of large corporations and high-income individuals caused a spontaneous excess of money. In contrast, in Japan today, the money game is based on the financial loosening adopted as a countermeasure against the potential effects of the strengthening of the yen and the weakening of the dollar. (Such a policy reaction came only after the third phase of the great depression in the United States.)

Such a spontaneous accumulation of excess money and the resultant money games can end abruptly. For example, the durable consumption boom passed its peak in June 1929, and manufacturing production in the United States began to fall; that is, the business cycle had already begun to turn down even before the collapse of stock prices. This development had already begun to lower the curtain on the excess money conditions and the money games. The crash was simply waiting to happen.

The governors of the Federal Reserve system realized the unstable nature of the boom, and attempted to suppress the explosion in stock prices by raising the discount rate several times during 1928 and 1929, from 3.5 percent in January 1928 to 6 percent in August 1929. But the consequent reduction in the interest rate differential between the United States and the United Kingdom caused a worsening of the pound crisis, and in response the Bank of England raised its discount rate from 5.5 percent to 6.5 percent in September 1929. On October 24, so-called Black Thursday began with the stock market crash in the United States.

October 1929 to September 1931
The fall of the stock market reduced the value of personal assets, and the "wealth effect" caused a reduction in domestic demand. Moreover, because production had already

begun to fall before the stock market collapse, expectations concerning the business cycle became even more cautious and depressed investment further. As a result, the dropoff in production that had started autonomously four months earlier became steeper after the crash.

Policy officials at that time were regarding this as a normal business recession, and in fact it appeared very much like that. The Board of Governors of the Federal Reserve lowered the discount rate from 6.5 percent to 4.5 percent in November 1929. Thereafter the discount rate was lowered again to 2 percent in 1930 and to the extremely low level of 1.5 percent in 1931.

The discount rate reductions of 1930 and 1931 were a response to the first banking panic that had occurred in the period between November 1930 and January 1931. The main reason for this banking crisis was the default on loans collateralized by securities that accompanied the stock crash. But other reasons soon became important as well.

A second reason for the banking crisis was default on agricultural loans. As seen above, the decline in farm prices due to excess supply of agricultural products caused economic impoverishment in the primary-product-producing countries and an accumulation of debt. After October 1929 the reduction in imports in the United States due to the recession caused a further worsening in world markets for primary commodities. During 1930 sacrifice sales of primary products by the indebted countries began, and market conditions worsened even further. As a result, domestic prices for primary products in the United States also deteriorated, and agriculture there was hurt even more seriously. The policy reaction to this situation was the enactment in July 1930 of the Smoot-Hawley tariffs, which raised tariffs on primary products. Even though the United

States, as the world's largest creditor country, was in a position to save the world economy, it chose to raise tariffs in order to protect its own farmers and thus worsened the worldwide agricultural panic. This process lit the fire on the second fuse for the credit crisis.

Sparks from the second fuse lit the third. With the worldwide crash of agricultural prices, the primary producing countries, particularly in Latin America, defaulted one after another beginning in January 1931. These defaults bounced back on the United States and became the third reason for the banking crisis. But defaulting countries were not limited to those in Latin America; in Eastern Europe as well the worsening of the world agricultural crisis caused default. As a result there were bank failures in Austria in May 1931 and in Germany in June. In the latter in particular, there were domino-like bankruptcies of banks, and exchange controls were imposed the following July with a freeze on short-term liabilities of banks also implemented. This behavior of Germany in attempting to stop the outflow of short-term foreign capital caused conjectures that such policies might also spread to the United Kingdom, which was burdened with an overvalued pound. The result was a flight from the pound into gold by European countries. This crisis touched off a still deeper period in the world depression. The United Kingdom was not able to withstand these conversions of the pound into gold, and finally suspended the gold standard in September.

September 1931 to April 1933

With the suspension of the gold standard by the United Kingdom, the British pound began to float with respect to the U.S. dollar, which was still on the gold standard. The market for the pound fell from $4.86 per pound to $3.50 per pound, a depreciation of about 30 percent in a single stroke. At the same time, suspicion spread that the United

States would also suspend the gold standard, and the flight from dollars into gold intensified.

In reacting to these gold outflows the United States made a fatal policy mistake. The discount rate, which had been held at the very low rate of 1.5 percent in response to the banking crisis and domestic recession, was raised to 3.5 percent; at the same time an insufficient money supply was provided as monetary policy tightened. This monetary contraction to stem gold outflows was the factor that changed the business recession in the United States from rather normal levels into an abnormal, exceedingly long recession. Real economic activity such as production fell on a scale exceeding even the declines between October 1929 and September 1931. Moreover, the second wave of banking crises, which had started in June of 1931, continued until February 1932, and yet a third wave of banking crises began in October 1932 and lasted until March 1933. As a result, in the following month the United States was unable to withstand pressure on its gold reserves, and it too suspended the gold standard. With this move, the discount rate was once again lowered to 1.5 percent in stages, and the misalignment between the dollar and the pound ended, putting a stop to this source of instability. This record-breaking business cycle downturn that lasted 43 months, starting in August 1929, bottomed out in March 1933. The recovery began in April 1933 as the suspension of the gold standard by the United States was announced. The worldwide panic was finally at an end.

Part of the responsibility for the extremely long, severe recession that began autonomously in the United States thus lay in a major policy failure, the tightening of monetary policy that occurred between September 1931 and April 1933. This policy ignored domestic economic conditions and took too much account of external considerations such as gold outflow.

Lessons of the Great Depression

The stock market collapse of October 1929 was a reflection of the autonomous recession at the end of a boom, and therefore cannot itself be called a cause of the world depression that continued for 43 months. The real causes were defects in the international economic system of the time. In thinking about the possibility of a recurrence of a worldwide depression, one must consider whether the defects in the international economic system of that time are once again latent in the system today.

Defects in the system

The defects in the international economic system that brought about the worldwide depression may be summarized as follows. They are traceable to the change in the world's largest creditor nation: the United Kingdom could no longer maintain the stability of the international economic system, while at the same time the United States did not realize that only it had the power to maintain stability. Nor did the United States attempt to assume the burden of responsibility. This situation manifested itself in the following ways.

First, the suspension of the gold standard by the United Kingdom in September 1931 was an act that itself demonstrated that the United Kingdom no longer had the power to maintain its position at the center of the international monetary system as the world's key currency country. The United States, at the same time, did not have the reserves to take over this task. Indeed, the United States became confused and implemented counterproductive policies such as financial tightening. These moves invited a worsening of business conditions at home, intensification of the worldwide agricultural depression, and a worldwide expansion of credit panics.

In retrospect, it is clear that the strong new key currency country of the United States should have loosened monetary policy and maintained low interest rates not only to prevent a fall of the old key currency, the pound, but also to stimulate domestic business conditions as soon as possible. If gold outflows were deemed undesirable, then, rather than raise interest rates, the dollar parity vis-à-vis gold should have been lowered immediately or the convertibility of the dollar into gold should have been suspended and a floating system introduced.

A second policy failure concerned several central banks. When bank failures began, the central banks of the world should have fulfilled their lender-of-last-resort function more quickly than they did in order to prevent the domino-like spread of credit panics. It is the destiny of central banks to save commercial banks by lending to them when the problem in these banks is not solvency but rather liquidity shortage. However, the Federal Reserve did not act as a lender of last resort in the round of credit panics that broke out in November 1930, and allowed a sharp reduction in deposits due to loss of confidence in the banking system. The Federal Reserve thus watched passively while a shrinkage of the money supply deepened the recession. In fact, the Federal Reserve worsened the credit panics by switching to a tight money policy in September 1931. On an international level, the central banks of the world scarcely cooperated at all as the credit panics spread. The Bank of England in particular was continuously passive about emergency financing related to credit panics on the Continent, such as those in Austria and Germany.

A third policy failure was that the United States, which had become the world's largest creditor nation due to payments surpluses, was wholly unconcerned with maintenance of the free trade system or with recycling its surpluses back to the rest of the world. Indeed, the United States wished to protect its own agricultural sector and raised tariffs on primary products, thus worsening the demand/supply balance in agriculture in the world as a whole and intensifying the agricultural depression. Moreover, capital outflows from the United States focused on portfolio investments that sought high returns and therefore were extraordinarily volatile. This development created further difficulties for debtor nations. The total lack of concern and irresponsibility of the United States with respect to the world economic conferences of 1933 speaks volumes about the conditions of that time.

The fact that the newly emergent largest creditor nation of that time, which was in a position to support the stability of the world economic system, was unconcerned with this destiny was the prime cause of the world depression. The end result of this economic isolationism was the separation of the world economy into blocs, the emergence of militarism, and the outbreak of the Second World War.

The importance of international cooperation and the role of Japan
These three failures teach pertinent lessons about the problems of today. The major lesson is that a repetition of the world depression is clearly preventable if efforts are made to maintain the stability of the world economic system through international cooperation, and if Japan, now the world's largest creditor nation, plays a specific role.

As mentioned earlier in this chapter, the scenarios of a return of the world depression today start with a collapse of the U.S. dollar. However, in an attempt to prevent such a dollar collapse, steps have already been taken through such policy cooperation as outlined in the Louvre Accord of February 1987 and in the Venice Summit communiqué in June of that year, in which the G-7 countries agreed to joint exchange market intervention and to an expansion of domestic demand in surplus countries and fiscal consolidation in deficit countries. Such international coordination proved effective in preventing the collapse of the dollar after the stock market crash of October 1987 and into early 1988, when the dollar threatened to crash.

The impact of a dollar collapse today would be much smaller than that of the collapse of the pound after suspension of the gold standard by the United Kingdom in September 1931. At that time, the overvaluation of the pound was ended in one stroke with a 30 percent devaluation. In contrast, the correction of the overvaluation of the dollar began with the Plaza Accord in September 1985 and has continued since then, reaching about 40 percent by 1988. Because the United States has become the world's largest debtor nation and has continued current account deficits on a large scale, pressure may build for a further fall in the value of the dollar. But precisely because of the flexible exchange rate system, there is not likely to be a buildup of pressure toward a dollar collapse, unlike the case of the collapse of the pound in 1931 under the fixed-rate, gold standard system. Today, pressures are relieved as they arise, so that further changes in the value of the dollar will most likely be small and gradual.

Moreover, even if the United States becomes lazy in its efforts to reduce its fiscal deficit in the aftermath of the 1988 presidential election, and if, as a result, the foreign payments deficit worsens and thus causes a collapse of the dollar, it is nevertheless highly unlikely that this collapse will develop into a world depression. First, because there is no gold standard today, it is absolutely unthinkable that Japan and the Federal Republic of Germany (and the EMS countries of Europe with it) would adopt the foolish policy of raising interest rates in order to stop gold outflows. If any actions were caused by such an event, there would be reductions of interest rates and the implementation of joint intervention in the exchange markets to buy dollars. These responses by Japan and the Federal Republic of Germany actually occurred in October 1987 when the world faced the danger of a dollar collapse following the stock market crash in New York. Therefore, a serious worsening of the domestic economic situation in these countries, such as occurred in the United States after September 1931, would not be caused by policies in either Japan or the Federal Republic of Germany. If there is a danger, it would be the outbreak of inflation as a result of the money growth associated with intervention. Moreover, the international transmission of the spillover effects of monetary policy is small under the floating exchange rate system today; therefore, even if interest rates were raised in one country, such increases would affect business conditions only in that country, and not spread to other countries.

In the case of the United States in the earlier period, the shock of the collapse of the pound occurred at a time at which the economy was exhausted from the continuation of an autonomous recession that had lasted for two years beginning in July 1929. Today, however, in the case of Japan, the high-yen recession has been overcome and business conditions are strong. A small fall of the dollar would not lead to a reversal of the cycle.

A third important difference between the depression era and today is that fiscal policy today plays the role of supporting business conditions. Macroeconomic policies, including fiscal policy, have considerable effect in offsetting the shocks from the strengthening of the yen and the weakening of the dollar.

Thus, it is unlikely that there will be a collapse of the dollar; even if there were, there is no possibility that such a collapse would bring about a deep recession in Japan or Europe. Moreover, it is important to remember that a depression differs from a recession. In a depression there are major disruptions of the economy and long-term stagnation occurs. For the three reasons mentioned above, even a dollar collapse would not be likely to bring about a depression. At most, there might be a recession of business cycle conditions that would be temporary.

One other question, however, requires examination: whether a collapse of the dollar would occasion an agricultural panic and credit panics such as occurred in the 1930s. In the world today, oil plays a role similar to that of agricultural products earlier. However, the excess production of petroleum has already peaked, and petroleum prices bottomed out in the middle of 1986. Moreover, international commodity markets in general have begun to recover from the disinflationary trend that occurred in the first half of the 1980s. This factor also represents an important difference from the situation in the 1930s.

Nevertheless, the debt problem of the oil-producing developing countries today is extremely serious. There are concerns that the difficulties of these developing countries in repaying both interest and principal on loans would combine with the money game in world financial markets to cause declines in both equity and bond markets and therefore invite bank bankruptcies. If this occurs, then there will be system risks that emerge in concert with the computerization and globalization of financial markets, leading to fears of credit panics as well. There are also issues of whether the world's largest creditor nation, Japan, will recycle its large trade surpluses through stable outflows and whether it will open its markets appropriately.

In addition, the boom in Japanese stocks is rather different in nature from that which occurred in the United States in the 1920s. In the United States then, the money game was based on an autonomous boom that accompanied an overheating of business conditions, and therefore the stock collapse itself was an autonomous reaction. In contrast, the money game in Japan today is the result of extremely liquid monetary conditions, and is likely to die down as these conditions return to the normal high-liquidity conditions that accompany the upswing of the business cycle. At that time, a market based on the improved performance of corporations is likely to re-emerge, so that, even if a correction does occur, there will not be a collapse of the market as there was in the United States in October 1929.

In preventing the recurrence of a world depression, Japan's role will be very great. Japan's first responsibility is to recycle its large surpluses in a stable fashion and to prevent a collapse of the dollar in addition to playing a substantial role in preventing defaults of loans by highly indebted countries. Japan's second responsibility is to maintain stable domestic growth based primarily on internal demand, even in the face of external shocks. This is a central role in the prevention of a simultaneous worldwide recession. To this end, very careful macro policies must be implemented in order to avoid both recession and inflation. In addition, calling forth the underlying equilibrium recovery power of Japanese industry that has existed hitherto is important. Also essential are structural policies, as discussed in Chapter 12, that will maintain the competitive power of firms and support the will to work of the population. Japan's third responsibility is to be active in making the Japanese yen and Japanese money and capital markets useful for the rest of the world, in order to help support the stability of the international monetary and financial systems—which are the subject of the next chapter.

4

Japan's Role
in the Future Monetary System

The Historical Role of Creditor Nations

The world in the late 1980s stands at an important historical turning point, that of a change in the world's largest
creditor nation. In the nineteenth century the United Kingdom became the world's largest creditor by continuing to
accumulate large trade surpluses, as shown in Table 7.
Thereafter, the United Kingdom also earned large amounts
of investment income, added these to its trade surpluses,
and finally ran very large current account surpluses. By
reinvesting these surpluses throughout the world, the British
created a Pax Britannica and became a world leader not
only in economics and politics but also in military and cultural affairs.

At that time, the gold standard was the foundation of
the monetary system and was supported by the gold reserves
of the United Kingdom, the largest creditor nation. The
British pound had guaranteed convertibility into gold, making it the most trustworthy of the gold-convertible currencies. The pound therefore functioned as the key currency

111

Table 7   Historical export/import ratios for the United Kingdom, the
United States, and Japan [(Exports/Imports) × 100].

Year	United Kingdom	United States	Japan
1820	151	118	–
30	151	118	–
40	173	130	–
50	–	82	–
60	79	94	–
70, 75 (average)	78	92	50
80, 85	71	128	97
90, 95	73	109	91
1900, 05	70	149	68
10–19	75[1]	153[2]	101[2]
20–29	72	125	85
30–39	59	115	100
40–49	53	232	–
50–59	81	136	76
60–69	85	119	94
70–79	84	92	104
80–84	95	82	109
85–86	89	58	149
87	85	59	154

Sources: Based on Bank of Japan, *Hundred Year Statistics of the Japanese
Economy* 1966; tables on customs clearance trade. For recent
years, International Monetary Fund, *International Financial
Statistics*.

Notes: 1. Average of 1910–1915.
2. Average of 1910–1920.

for the world. The financial and capital markets in the
City of London were international markets denominated
in the British pound and were, so to speak, international
public goods. Trade, financial, and capital transactions
throughout the world developed in large part due to the
existence of these public goods under the hegemony of the
United Kingdom.

At the end of the nineteenth century, however, two other
countries emerged as creditor nations on the basis of con-

tinuous trade balance surpluses: Germany and the United States. These two countries, however, did not open their internal markets and had no intention of supplying their own national financial and capital markets as international public goods. One result of these developments was the outbreak of the First World War, as a conflict between the United Kingdom and Germany. Even though the war left Germany defeated and Britain exhausted, the new great creditor nation, the United States, still did not wish to play the role of an international provider of public goods. In the end, the domestically oriented policies pursued by the United States contributed to the great depression, as seen in the previous chapter. With this depression, the world economy separated into protectionist blocs in the 1930s, and the fuse of confrontations that would eventually explode in the Second World War was lit.

The change of the world's largest creditor nation from the United Kingdom to the United States in the first half of the twentieth century was a decisive moment in world history. It provided the context for the Bretton Woods conference to plan the postwar monetary system, at which the Keynes Plan promoted by the United Kingdom lost to the White Plan of the United States. The Bretton Woods system of the postwar period was thus created, with its two main pillars being a gold exchange standard with the U.S. dollar as the key currency and fixed but adjustable exchange rates. The U.S. dollar and the New York financial and capital markets thus began to function as international public goods. The international economic order had the IMF Agreement and the GATT Treaty at its center, and the United States established hegemony in political, military, and cultural affairs. Pax Americana was the order of the day.

The United States has now become the world's largest debtor nation. Its current account deficit in 1987 was 160

Table 8. Net foreign assets and liabilities of Japan and the United
States (in $ billions)

Year	Japan			United States		
	Assets (A)	Liabilities (B)	Net position (A − B)	Assets (A)	Liabilities (B)	Net position (A − B)
1973	47.6	34.5	13.0	222.8	174.9	47.9
74	55.9	47.0	8.9	255.7	196.9	58.8
75	58.3	51.3	7.0	295.1	220.9	74.3
76	68.0	58.4	9.6	347.2	263.6	83.6
77	80.1	58.1	22.0	379.1	306.4	72.7
78	118.7	82.5	36.2	447.8	371.7	76.1
79	135.4	106.6	28.8	510.6	416.1	94.5
80	159.6	148.0	11.5	606.9	500.8	106.0
81	209.3	198.3	10.9	719.7	579.0	140.7
82	227.7	203.0	24.7	824.9	688.1	136.9
83	272.0	234.7	37.3	873.9	784.5	89.4
84	341.2	266.9	74.3	896.1	892.6	3.5
85	437.7	307.9	129.8	950.3	1,061.0	−110.7
86	727.3	547.0	180.4	1,071.4	1,340.7	−269.2
87	1,071.6	830.9	240.7	1,167.8	1,536.0	−368.2

billion dollars, and its year-end net debtor position exceeded
368 billion dollars, as shown in Table 8. Although the ac-
curacy of this 368 billion dollar figure is open to question
since it is unadjusted for capital gains on assets, the United
States in any case will be a net debtor in 1988 since its 1988
balance on net investment income will be in deficit. Even
if the current account deficit shrinks in 1988 and after,
as expected, the accumulation of debts will continue
until this deficit reaches zero. And even if the fiscal deficit
that lies behind these current account deficits shrinks
in line with the targets set by the new Gramm-Rudman-
Hollings Amendment, it is unreasonable to expect that the
capital inflow and the current account deficits will be eliminated before the mid-1990s. Moreover, the rapid reduction
in fiscal deficits outlined in the new law in fact appear

difficult to achieve, so that as interest payments on net debt accumulate, there is a corresponding probability that the current account deficits will continue for some time to come. If this is in fact the case, then in the 1990s the United States will have a net debtor position in excess of 1 trillion dollars. Relative to the very large GNP of the United States this net debtor position is small, however, when compared with those of the debtor nations of Latin America in the 1980s. At the same time the United States remains the key currency country. What will happen to the international monetary order when a key currency country with a trillion dollars worth of debt tries to solve its fiscal problems? Like an elephant in a rowboat, even the slightest movements of the U.S. economy in pursuing adjustment policies will be reflected in movements of the international monetary order as a whole, through the effects of confidence in the key currency. This was precisely the case in October 1987 when a rise in U.S. interest rates, initiated to prevent a fall in the dollar, triggered worldwide financial turmoil, starting with the stock market crash in New York.

Pax Japonica?
The experiences and lessons of history show, as described in the previous chapter, that when a new creditor nation comes onto the scene without opening its own markets and without thinking about its own macroeconomic policy from the viewpoint of the world economy, severe conflicts can occur between the new and old powers, with wars, depressions, or separation of the world economy into protectionist blocs. The intensification of economic friction and the emergence of protectionism among major countries today suggest the possibility that such crises might recur if Japan fails to act appropriately.

An obvious question to ask is whether Japan, which has now become the world's largest creditor nation, should aim to establish an international monetary system focusing on the yen and establish Pax Japonica. The answer to this question is clearly no.

The move from the hegemony of the United Kingdom to that of the United States took about half a century. Although the United States is now the world's largest debtor nation, it is much too early to tell whether this situation will continue for the next half-century and whether the United States will lose its leadership ability in the international scene in economic, political, military, and cultural affairs. At the same time, although Japan has become the world's largest creditor nation, this is a phenomenon of only a few years, as shown in Tables 7 and 8. Whether this situation will continue, and whether Japan can show leadership in the international arena in political, military, and cultural affairs, is entirely unknown. In military affairs, in particular, such a role is neither possible nor desirable.

More decisive, however, will probably be the fact that the world will become far more multilateral in nature in the coming century, and it will not be possible for any single country to establish hegemony. Indeed, the lack of a likely hegemonic power is not traceable to simplistic notions of conflict between North and South or East and West; rather, within each area many conflicts are already in existence. The hegemony of the United States within the West and that of the Soviet Union in the East are already being reduced, while the Asian NIEs are leaving the South for the North and the People's Republic of China will strengthen its role as a major country in the next century.

What will succeed a Pax Americana is not a Pax Japonica but rather a multinational system of international coordination. Japan must think about how to provide international public goods actively within that framework. In the international monetary sphere, the U.S. dollar will cease being the sole key currency of the international monetary system;

in its place it will be necessary to seek a multilateral currency system focusing on the U.S. dollar, the Japanese yen, and the ECU (a weighted average of currencies in the European Monetary System, centering on the German mark). With such a multilateral system it will be possible to reduce, at least to some extent, the direct impact of economic fluctuations in the United States on the international monetary order as a whole.

The establishment of a multilateral currency system will not be like the establishment of the Bretton Woods system, i.e., through international treaty. Through the process of globalization of finance under the current floating exchange rate system, there will be a system of competition among the financial and currency markets of different countries, and a multilateral currency system will emerge as a natural result. Japan's destiny as the world's largest creditor nation is to compete in this system.

The yen as a key currency
Several years ago in Japan the common wisdom was that the yen should become neither an international currency nor (in particular) a settlement currency. If this were to occur, so the thinking went, some foreign countries would accumulate large yen holdings. Then, if the stability of the Japanese economy were seen to falter, people throughout the world might forecast inflation and balance of payments deficits in Japan and flee from the yen to other international currencies in an effort to avoid the currency losses that would accompany a sudden devaluation of the yen. Such movements would, of course, bring about a sudden devaluation and worsen the fluctuations of the Japanese economy. The British economy of the 1950s and the 1960s and the U.S. economy today in fact either did experience or are experiencing such difficulties.

Just because, however, there are such dangers associated

with countries that provide a key currency, this does not mean that Japan should refuse the yen such an international role. What would happen if Japan tried to avoid this role? First, criticism of Japan and its current account surpluses as a destabilizing factor in the world economy would certainly increase, and the nation would be increasingly isolated by the further emergence of protectionism in Europe and the United States. In contrast, if Japan opened its financial markets, systems, and traditions to international influence and continued to deregulate, then the Japanese current account surpluses would represent a stable supply of capital that incorporates the most advanced technologies. Japan would also be a source of lending of international currency. Only when Japanese financial and capital markets provide these international public goods will Japan be in harmony with the world economy. It is therefore necessary to think of the disadvantages of being a key currency country as a necessary cost. On the other hand, this cost must be paid only if the Japanese economy becomes destabilized through policy failures of its own. The critical point is not to make such errors.

From the viewpoint of Japan's national interests, it is desirable for the yen to become a key currency. One reason for this is that in the current circumstances, almost all of Japan's foreign assets are denominated in U.S. dollars and therefore immediately subject to risks of currency depreciation. It would be desirable for Japan to increase its proportion of yen-denominated international assets, or at least to shift to a currency basket formula that includes the U.S. dollar, the yen, and the European ECU.

In order, however, for the Japanese yen to play the role of a key currency, it is necessary to further internationalize the Tokyo financial and capital markets by promoting international standards in system operations, business practices, and regulations. It is therefore imperative to aim at a 24-hour financial and capital market that is completely globalized and tied through electronic networks to the New York and European markets. The New York market will focus on borrowing and lending in U.S. dollars while the Euromarkets centering on London will focus on offshore transactions among the U.S. dollar, Japanese yen, German mark, or other currencies, i.e., the same roles they have previously played. The Tokyo market will have two roles. One is to be the market for borrowing and lending in the new key currency of the yen; the other, to supply capital to developing countries.

A Sustainable Floating Exchange Rate System

The major concern about an international monetary system composed of several key currencies, i.e., the U.S. dollar, the yen, and the ECU (or German mark), is the potential for huge shifts of funds among the three currencies at times when the relative economic fundamentals of the U.S. economy, the Japanese economy, or the European economy are subject to change. Therefore, in order to function under a multicurrency international monetary system, it will be necessary to build in a mechanism that will minimize fluctuations of exchange rates among those three currencies.

One way to do this would be to fix the exchange rates of the three currencies within a narrow range, as is done among European currencies in the EMS. However, one reason why the EMS functions as well as it does on the European continent is that the member countries are rather similar in economic structure, with relatively small open economies organized together around the Federal Republic of Germany. It would be very difficult, however, to fix exchange rates among economies so different in character as the United States, Japan, and the Federal Republic of Germany. Historical experience suggests that fixed exchange rate systems function best under such systems as Pax Britannica or Pax Americana, when the hegemon is at the height of its power. The relatively smaller and weaker countries would fix their own currencies vis-à-vis those of larger countries with stable prices and large net creditor positions. When smaller countries run current account deficits that would tend to invalidate the fixed exchange rates, these countries would attempt to solve the problem with domestic policy measures, and in cases where this is impossible, they would request permission from the others to devalue. In the EMS today, this is precisely the arrangement adopted, and it appears to function well.

In the world in the late 1980s, however, when a hegemonic power has ceased to exist and multilateralization has progressed, it would be impossible to create an international monetary system of fixed exchange rates among the three key currencies. Moreover, experience since the early 1970s has shown that the flexible exchange rate system was able to weather two major oil crises. As shown at that time, the move toward simultaneous fluctuation and destabilization in the economies of the major countries over those years was not traceable to the nature of the floating exchange rate system.

The experience under floating exchange rates
In considering the desirable form of the international monetary system of the future, it is helpful to recall the experiences and lessons of floating exchange rates.

First, the floating exchange rate period saw a greater degree of freedom in macroeconomic policymaking compared with that under the fixed exchange rate system. Countries were able to implement appropriate macroeconomic policies of their own volition, so that it was easier than under the fixed exchange rate system to plan for the economic stability of an individual country. The macroeconomies of certain countries seemed to become less stable and more simultaneous in their movements after the shift to floating exchange rates, not because policy freedom was lower, but rather because two oil crises and the consequent worldwide recession hit all these countries at the same time, and because national policy officials reacted more or less in the same way. The oil crises themselves had no direct relationship to the floating exchange rate system, and in fact were exogenous. If anything, the occurrence of the oil crises can be attributed to some extent to the character of the fixed exchange rate system. From the late 1960s through the early 1970s, the United States ran increasing current account deficits which accumulated gold and foreign currency reserves of other nations with dollars, the sole key currency under the fixed-rate regime. This caused overly expansionary policies in most countries, with a resultant increase in the relative price of manufactured goods in terms of commodities, and hence set the stage for the process of sharp catch-up increases in world commodity prices which focused in its later phase on oil.

If the emphasis on price stability under this floating exchange rate system continues, it is unlikely that the events of the late 1960s and early 1970s will be repeated. Therefore, there would seem to be less of a possibility for the recurrence of a major oil crisis in the form of a large-scale increase in prices, although the price of oil may gradually rise over the next decade.

Another conclusion that can be drawn from experience under the floating exchange rate system is that the countries that succeeded in keeping inflation relatively low against a background of stable management of monetary policy (Japan, the Federal Republic of Germany, and France) were able to maintain fluctuations in their economic growth rates and inflation rates at relatively low levels despite the common experience of oil crises, as shown in Table 5 of Chapter 1. Growth rates fluctuated more in the United States and in the United Kingdom. In this sense, the stabilization of prices in the leading industrial countries not only lowers the possibility of a recurrence of oil crises, but also suggests that the effects of such crises on the real economies of countries would be smaller if they did occur.

A second lesson from the floating exchange rate period is that short-term fluctuations of exchange rates are unavoidable with active international capital movements. Any attempt to revive fixed exchange rates through market intervention would soon show intervention to be powerless in the face of large, speculative capital movements. Moreover, any attempts to regulate capital movements through taxation such as a Tobin tax or through regulation in an effort to stabilize markets would quickly be undone, even if temporarily successful. This is because loopholes would quickly be found and would reduce the effectiveness of such policies. The existence of loopholes, however, would be a source of disturbance that is both inefficient and unfair. They might also suppress the stabilization of speculation and could even become a source of instability. Risk avoidance for short-term fluctuations can be achieved through forward transactions and lending and borrowing transactions. Therefore, market intervention in an attempt to eliminate such short-term exchange rate fluctuations and to revive fixed exchange rates not only would be ineffective, but probably would even be unnecessary.

A third lesson learned under floating exchange rates is that, as was shown in Figure 5, real exchange rates, calculated using either the GNP deflator or the wholesale price index for industrial products, have exhibited a level trend in the long term. This implies that exchange rates have moved largely in line with purchasing power parity over the long term. On the other hand, deviations from purchasing power parity have at some times lasted for several years, so in this sense the exchange market is unstable—in that it is not clear when purchasing power parity rates will reassert themselves. These deviations from purchasing power parity have been caused largely by movements of real interest rate differentials among countries and the risk premiums associated with cumulative current account positions. In addition, for countries with large fluctuations in their inflation rates, such as the United States and the United Kingdom, it is difficult to predict exactly what the correct purchasing power parity rates are, because of price instability. When movements of purchasing power are difficult to predict, the rates of exchange among fiat currencies, which are not backed by real commodities, are fundamentally indeterminate and therefore will move very easily. In fact, the real exchange rates among low-inflation countries like Japan and the Federal Republic of Germany have fluctuated less than the real exchange rates vis-à-vis countries with variable inflation like the United States. In addition, the deviations of exchange rates from purchasing power parity have been lower among the low-inflation countries. This may be because future parity is easier to predict.

Because deviations in exchange rates from purchasing power parity imply that the law of one price does not hold internationally, such deviations will, if they continue for some time, bring about inefficiencies in the international allocation of resources and hinder economic development in the world as a whole. It is therefore desirable that exchange rates remain near purchasing power parity levels in the medium term, even within a system of floating exchange rates.

A fourth lesson of the floating exchange rate period is that even when exchange rates remain at purchasing power parity levels in the medium and long terms, there can still be imbalances in current accounts. This is because savings rates and investment opportunities differ from one country to another. In particular, in countries in which the ratio of the fiscal deficit to GNP is moving in a particular direction, the current account balance will also move. Among the United States, Japan, and the Federal Republic of Germany in the 1980s, large current account imbalances emerged because of such factors and brought with them various problems, including a revival of protectionism and trade frictions. In theory, specialization in production and export together with perfect mobility of international capital represent an appropriate allocation of resources and should not be adjusted. However, if major countries cannot sustain the resulting imbalances for political reasons, countering the political problems of protectionism and trade friction becomes a task of primary importance.

Policy Coordination in a Desirable Monetary Order

The floating exchange rate period taught us four lessons. First, there has been an expansion of macroeconomic independence, which implies responsibility on the part of each country for its own price stability. Second, short-term fluctuations of exchange rates are both unavoidable and permissible. Market intervention to stabilize exchange rate movements at a certain level is ineffective. The third lesson is the importance of purchasing power parity (PPP) rates as an anchor for medium- and long-term exchange rate movements and the importance of domestic price stability in minimizing deviations of exchange rates from these PPP rates. Fourth, even with relatively stable PPP rates, there remains the potential for major imbalances in current accounts based on differences in savings rates and investment opportunities in different countries. Although such imbalances represent a good allocation of resources, they can cause serious political problems.

On the basis of these four lessons, let us now consider

the future international monetary order and the role of international policy coordination. First, it is important to construct a multilateral currency system based on maintenance of the framework of the floating exchange rate system. Within this framework, however, it would not be desirable if there were continuous medium-term swings in the exchange rates of several key currencies. It is therefore necessary to construct an international framework which will minimize to the greatest extent possible the medium-term fluctuation of the exchange rates between the key currencies, while maintaining the principle of the floating exchange rate system—that is, without market intervention to fix a certain range.

There are two levels of problems which need to be solved in constructing such a system. On one level, it is necessary to achieve international agreement on the values around which movements in the medium-term exchange rates should be stabilized. The major question is whether these values should be those at which current accounts will be brought into balance or those at which purchasing power parity holds. In our 16 years of experience with floating exchange rates, deviations from purchasing power parity over the long term have not, in general, occurred, as seen in Figure 5. In this sense, the law of one price has operated correctly at an international level. But these same 16 years of experience give no guarantee that such exchange rates will bring about current account balances. Even if the law of one price holds, current account imbalances may continue on the basis of savings-investment differentials. There is no doubt theoretically that the purchasing power parity rate is better for the allocation of international resources than the rates that bring current accounts into balance.

At another level, there needs to be agreement on the implementation of international cooperation in order to

minimize the deviation of exchange rates from the desired
levels. If these levels correspond to purchasing power parity
rates, then policy cooperation will be relatively easy. All
that would be required would be to choose a particular
price index (the GNP deflator or the wholesale price index
for common tradeable goods using international trade
weights for a basket of those goods) and a base period
(some time in the 1970s), and then the anchor to minimize
the medium-term fluctuation of exchange rates would be
determined.

If, however, the levels are those that would balance
the current accounts, policy cooperation will be a more
difficult problem, in both economic and political terms.
Various problems may arise because setting such levels for
exchange rates on the basis of economic calculations is extremely difficult. There could exist any number of possible
exchange rates consistent with this goal, even at a given
level of purchasing power parity, depending upon differences between countries in terms of macroeconomic policies
and economic structures. In other words, these anchor exchange rates are sensitive to anything that affects the savings
rates and investment opportunities of the countries involved.
Thus the desired levels around which exchange rates should
fluctuate in the medium run would be contingent on the
economic policies of countries which influence domestic
savings and investment—fiscal, tax, and industrial policy,
for example. Associated with such calculations are two
problems that are virtually insoluble.

The first problem is that consensus on anchor rates would
require a common economic model that expresses the relationships between exchange rates, current accounts, and
policy mixes, and that also links national economies through
complex mutual dependence relationships. At the current
state of the art in economics, however, there exists neither
a theoretical model nor an econometric model that ade-

quately simulates with sufficient generality the relationships among such endogenous variables as exchange rates, prices, interest rates, current account balances, and GNP, on the one hand, and such exogenous variables as policy variables and economic or tax structure, on the other. The models that do exist make bold assumptions, and only shed light on certain aspects of the transmission channels of economic effects between countries. Thus, the appropriate exchange rates derived will differ according to the model used. If each country uses a model that suits its own purposes, conflicts of international interest will occur.

A second problem in calculating such exchange rates is that, even if consensus can be reached on a common econometric model, reaching a consensus on economic policies might imply relinquishing sovereignty over broad policy aspects, including fiscal, tax, and industrial policies. Such a move would be impossible politically and inappropriate economically. The reason for the latter is that perfect balance in the current accounts of countries is not necessarily a guarantee of appropriate international allocation of resources. A more appropriate allocation of resources could be achieved even with current account imbalances if exchange rates were at levels corresponding to purchasing power parity.

Based on these considerations, therefore, it would appear that the appropriate levels for the medium-term anchor for minimizing exchange rate movements would be the rates that correspond to purchasing power parity.

Independence of national monetary policy
Our 16 years of experience under the floating exchange rate system indicate that exchange rates do in fact behave according to purchasing power parity rates over the long term. (Cases in which there was deviation from these rates on a trend basis were exceptions, such as the case of the

British pound, which saw the terms of trade improve because of the development of the North Sea oil fields.) In particular, in the years just after the first oil crisis, until inflation on a worldwide scale was stabilized around 1977, real exchange rates among the U.S. dollar, the Japanese yen, and the German mark were fairly stable, implying that they tended to move in concert with purchasing power parity even in the short term, as shown in Figure 5 in Chapter 2. Thus, in the future, if the major countries adopt of their own volition appropriate monetary policies and thereby stabilize inflation at low levels, then the exchange rates among their currencies will more easily move without deviating much from purchasing power parity levels because market participants can easily foresee the future course of PPP. The 16 years of experience under floating rates also suggest that the countries that attempted to stabilize monetary growth rates in the floating rate period, that is, Japan, the Federal Republic of Germany, and France, were more successful in their inflation stabilization performance than they had been during the fixed exchange rate period. The Japanese case is quite instructive; please refer again to Figure 1 in Chapter 1. In Japan, money growth has been more stable under the floating rate system than under fixed rates. As a result, real growth rates have been more stable, and inflation rates have also been constrained at a low level.

Non-monetary policies to eliminate current account imbalances

Even if monetary policy under a floating exchange rate system could bear the double burden of maintaining price stability and holding exchange rates in the neighborhood of purchasing power parity, it could not also assume the responsibility of ensuring current account balance. Even if the law of one price were to hold on an international level with exchange rates at purchasing power parity, there would be no guarantee of current account balance. Nor can one forget that monetary policy, in contrast to fiscal policy, has indeterminate and perhaps small effects on current account balances. In other words, the spillover effect of monetary policy is very small. Therefore, if major countries cannot allow a current accounts imbalance for political reasons, policies other than monetary policy should be directed toward correcting the imlabance.

Under the floating rate system, opposite fiscal policy stances between one country and another often generated both differentials in real interest rates and expansions of current account imbalances due to differences in domestic absorption. These resulted in exchange rates deviating from purchasing power parity over periods of several years through widening of real interest differentials. Moreover, the expansion of current account imbalances in fact stimulated protectionism in the United States and threatened world free trade. For such political reasons, it is important to pursue international policy coordination (including fiscal policy) in order to prevent the emergence and expansion of "extreme" current account imbalances.

Because of the deep-seated relationship between fiscal policy and domestic political issues, however, it is impossible to achieve policy coordination in its most complete form. This is the essence of the problem of national sovereignty mentioned above. Still, if political leaders of major countries were to meet and discuss these issues, they would better realize the international effects that individual countries' policies have and would gain a more precise understanding of the economic conditions and policy stances of other countries. As a result, it might even be possible to accommodate by making policy adjustments.

One example of such policy coordination can be seen in the efforts of the United States to cut its fiscal expenditures and the corresponding efforts of Japan and the Federal Republic of Germany to expand theirs. Narrowing the current account imbalance is not the final goal of economic policy, but an intermediate target to prevent threats to free trade.

Over the somewhat longer term, different policies are called for in different countries to narrow the current account imbalance. In the United States, it appears necessary to pursue investment promotion policies that will strengthen international competitiveness and also to devise policies to raise savings. In Japan, as was noted in the 1986 Maekawa Report, it would seem necessary to deregulate and to open domestic markets further in order to shift the economy from dependence on high exports and low imports to greater dependence on high domestic demand and increased imports. These issues are extremely broad in scope and would not at first seem to be topics for international policy coordination precisely because they seem to relate to national sovereignty. It is important to counter this narrow attitude by creating international forums for discussion, by determining the international impact of economic policies in a broad sense (including structural reform), and by seeking avenues of policy coordination that will help to maintain and enhance free trade.

The global financial market and the functioning of a multilateral currency system
Policy coordination will be one of the major underpinnings for the multilateral currency system, and within that system each of the key currencies will have a separate function.

In general, any currency has three functions, i.e., means of payment, unit of account, and store of value. The key currencies in an international monetary system also have all these three functions. For example, the U.S. dollar is used as the means of payment for most types of international transactions and also as the unit of account for international transactions—U.S. dollar-denominated contracts are by far the most common. As a store of value, the role of the U.S. dollar is also great, for example, in the holding of official currency reserves of various countries in U.S. dollar-denominated assets or in the holding of foreign exchange reserves of corporations in U.S. dollar assets. However, in the future, the globalization of finance is expected to continue, along with the setting of international standards for regulation. As part of this process, there will be a marked change in the roles of currencies if, as expected, it becomes much easier to redenominate the currency of transactions.

First of all, in the globalized financial market of the future, it will be easy to conduct 24-hour trading across a broad spectrum of currencies in various instruments such as futures, currency swaps, and options trading. As a result, the necessity for a single key currency is likely to decline, and thus reliance on the currency of the largest debtor nation—that is, on the U.S. dollar— will probably weaken. As this occurs, the Japanese yen will come to share the role of key currency, as financial and technical conditions for a multi-key currency system come about. In particular, among the three functions of a currency, that of means of payment will no longer necessarily have to be filled by a single key currency. This is because any of the key currencies could be converted with complete safety and at very low cost into any other currency. The costs of re-denomination between currencies would become very low.

The degree of choice among currencies should also decrease, because of the possibility of hedging for minimizing both currency risk and interest rate risk. However, because hedging over long periods of time involves larger costs, there will likely be a tendency to prefer the currency of the country with the most stable economy as a store of value for international transactions, for reserve holdings, and so on. There is therefore the possibility that the most useful reserve currency within the multilateral currency system will be that of the country or area that exhibits the greatest stability of macroeconomic performance.

Finally, considering the function of unit account, which is the basis for longer-term contracts denominated in a currency, there would seem to be the possibility of a more widespread use of basket formulas (such as the European ECU) involving several key currencies as a means for diversifying risk. In addition to the ECU, there is another basket, the SDR, issued by the International Monetary Fund. The ECU now has a track record of being actually used as a contract currency for long-term financial transactions, whereas the SDR has no such record. This is probably because the ECU uses weights that are related to international trade and therefore reflect rather accurately the currency markets of the member countries of the EMS. In the SDR, the weight of the dollar is rather high, and therefore the SDR tends to depreciate with the dollar. It thus seems desirable to work toward constructing a basket that will accurately reflect the movements of the U.S. dollar, the yen, and the ECU according to their weights in international transactions.

The Trend toward Yen-denominated Horizontal Trade in Asia

Japan for the first time in its history has reached the stage at which horizontal trade with neighboring Asian countries has become possible. Since the Meiji Restoration, Japan has engaged in so-called vertical trade. Japanese firms imported raw materials and processed them into finished products, which were in turn exported. As a result, Japan has structurally run trade deficits with such resource-exporting countries as Oceanian and Middle Eastern countries, while running surpluses with the developed economies of North America and Europe which provided export markets for Japan. This vertical trade structure determined by resource endowment partly explains the chronic nature of the trade friction between Japan and such trade partners as the United States.

However, this century-old traditional trade structure is beginning to change. The share of finished goods in total Japanese imports exceeded 50 percent in September 1988, with increasing imports of manufactured goods from nearby Asian countries. In other words, mutual exchange of finished products, which can be called horizontal trade, is becoming more prominent than the traditional vertical trade.

There are two underlying reasons for this structural change. First, in addition to the NIEs, more ASEAN member nations have succeeded in developing industries mature enough to export finished products to Japan. Second, the substantial appreciation in value of the yen since September 1985 has created a new situation for the Japanese economy. Now, it is more economical for Japan to specialize in the export of advanced manufacturing products and to import other items from nearby Asian countries.

Meanwhile, what can be expected from this emerging change in Japan's trade structure? If we look ahead toward the 1990s and the early twenty-first century, there is a possibility that the third largest horizontal trade area in the free world will be formed in Asia. This trade area, involving Japan and other Asian countries, would be next in size to two other such areas: the American continent (comprising the U.S., Canada, and Latin America) and Western Europe.

In the 1980s, the largest export market for Japan as well as for NIEs and the ASEAN nations is the United States, not other neighboring countries in Asia. Thus, Asia does not constitute a third horizontal trade area, but is subordinate to the horizontal trade area of the American continent. It may not be entirely out of the realm of possibility to envision a similar dependence of Asia on the American continent continuing into the twenty-first century.

Careful examination of trade statistics enables us to discern signs of emerging structural shifts. For example, in the total Japanese exports of $229 billion in 1987, the share of the United States still remained the largest at 37 percent, compared with the 23 percent share of Asia. However, in accounting for the increase of $20 billion from the previous year, the share of Asia was 56 percent, far exceeding the share of 16 percent for the United States. Similar changes can be observed for NIEs. While the United States absorbed 32 percent of the annual increase of their exports in 1987 compared with 17 percent for Japan, the difference between the share of the United States and the share of Japan in NIE exports has been narrowing rapidly since 1985. Indeed, the share of Japan finally exceeded that of the United States, by the margin of 22 versus 13 percent, in the first half of 1988.

The fact that Japan's share now exceeds the share of the United States in increased exports to Asia suggests that the share of Japan in total exports will eventually exceed that of the United States. Once we recognize that the above figures do not include intra-regional trade within Asia, the true underlying share of horizontal trade among Asian countries emerges as in fact much larger, and is thus likely to exceed the share of U.S. trade that much sooner.

Although the GNP of the United States is 1.6 times that of Japan, the United States depends less on trade than Japan: the value of Japanese exports in 1987 was 90 with the index of 100 for U.S. exports. On the import side, the value of U.S. imports was 167, reflecting the large trade deficit, relative to Japan's 59. Since it is about three times the Japanese market, the U.S. market seems to exert a dominating influence on Asian trade.

However, if the United States could reduce its twin deficits and if Japan could reduce its trade surplus by expanding domestic demand, the relative amount of imports by the two countries would converge toward the relative size of exports, that is, 100 versus 90. Moreover, if the yen appreciates further against the dollar, even a reversal of the relative size of imports is possible. It is also in this sense that a horizontal trade area in Asia with Japan at its center can emerge outside the United States.

Since the yen is the hardest currency in the world today, neighboring Asian countries are willing to denominate their exports to Japan in yen and to hold yen as reserves. As a matter of fact, the ratios both of yen-denominated exports to Japan and of yen held as reserves by Asian countries are now increasing rapidly, although they are still low compared to the corresponding dollar ratios. These trends are enhanced by the increase in Japan's yen-denominated capital exports to Asian countries, since they must accumulate yen reserves to repay their borrowings.

I believe that these structural changes suggest that a third horizontal trade area centering on Japan will take shape in Asia, and the role of the yen as an international currency for the region will increase in importance. These economic changes have been instrumental in forming my views on the future organization of the international monetary order.

5

The Steady Course of Financial Reform

One of the great historical issues facing Japan in the late 1980s is how to play an appropriate role in the international monetary system of the future in accordance with its new economic power, while promoting financial reform and adapting to the globalization of finance. This chapter will consider the current state and outlook for financial reform in Japan in comparison with the United States and other countries, and will consider related issues in some detail.

Financial Reform Today and in the Future

Financial reform began in Japan around 1973 with the collapse of the Bretton Woods system, the occurrence of the first oil crisis that ended the high-growth period, and the new historical environment under the floating exchange rate system. Along with these changes, four new economic and technological conditions fostered major changes in the financial world.

The first new condition was the large-scale flotations of government bonds that accompanied the shift to lower growth. An important result for these flotations was the expansion of open markets for both long- and short-maturity instruments that were free in terms of access and interest rate determination mechanism and that took such forms as the growth of the secondary market for long-term government bonds, the growth of the primary market for medium-term government bonds, and the expansion of the repurchase (*gensaki*) market. The second new condition was that corporations and individuals came to react quite sensitively to changes in liberalized interest rates. This new sensitivity occurred because both corporations and individuals began to pay much closer attention to the cost of borrowing and the interest rates on lending their funds, in response to pressures for leaner management and lower wage increases that accompanied the shift to low growth. Extra stimulus to these trends was provided by the increase in internal financial power of corporations and the accumulation of assets by individuals. The third new condition was the much more active trading of funds across international borders after the shift to the floating exchange rate system. The increase in such flows was due to higher incentives for international transactions in both yen and foreign currencies and followed the liberalization of capital transactions in principle unless specifically forbidden, codified under the 1980 Foreign Exchange Act revision. The fourth new condition was the large decrease in transaction costs of financial trading. This occurred due to the active introduction of communications and computer technology in the financial industry and the higher level of business expertise in asset and liability management.

Many countries had similar experiences in this regard. Indeed, these four new conditions were common to many industrial countries and formed the background for the movement toward financial innovations. They also brought an end to the complementarity between the various regulations and financial customs that had functioned effectively during the postwar recovery period and the high-growth period. The aspects of the financial system that illustrated the lack of complementarity between the new conditions and the old financial systems were the various interest rate regulations; the regulations on separation of fields of business, the various types of regulations that separated domestic and foreign markets (e.g., foreign exchange controls) in order to strengthen the effectiveness of the former regulations; the regulations and customs intended to preserve orderly credit conditions, such as the collateral principle for lending; and entry and exit regulations in the banking industry. In the following both the past history of and the outlook for the most important of these will be discussed.

Interest rate regulations and liberalization
Since all but a very small portion of lending rates and bond interest rates in Japan had been free rates, interest rate control in Japan was in essence the control of deposit interest rates. Interest rate controls on deposit rates were based on the experiences of the frequent financial crises that occurred from the start of the twentieth century up until the 1930s, and were originally introduced in the form of agreements among banks. In the postwar period, in order to preclude cartel-like behavior under such agreements, they were converted to legal regulations. During Japan's high-growth period, deposit rates were generally maintained at low levels. However, there was also a desire to promote investment and exports by keeping interest rates artificially low through the operation of such interest rate controls. This differs from the motivation in the United States, in which Regulation Q, although based on similar experiences of financial panic in the 1930s, was used as a supplementary tool in periods of monetary tightening and was also used to facilitate investment in housing.

With the shift from high to low growth, the importance of using interest controls as a policy tool weakened, but the controls themselves were continued. What vitiated the controls in the end were movements on the part of the private sector to avoid these regulations. An early example was the sharp increase during the mid-1970s in the use of repurchase transactions by securities companies, based on the markedly higher frequency of issues of government bonds. These transactions are similar to the repurchase transactions in the United States and involve, in a sense, the conversion of long-term government bonds (10 years) into short-term (3–6 months), fixed-interest bills. As corporations sought more efficient investment of their funds and avoidance of deposit rate controls, they shifted funds from short-term, fixed deposits to the repurchase market. Moreover, securities companies constructed a smaller denomination asset in the form of medium-term government bond funds, which were similar to money market mutual funds in the U.S. and were sold primarily to individuals. The Postal Savings Bank responded with instruments such as fixed-amount postal savings deposits that had attractive earnings and liquidity characteristics. As individuals strengthened their preference for high-yielding assets, funds shifted in large quantities into this instrument. As a result, regular deposit-taking financial institutions saw their share of total funds fall from the earlier value of 60 to 70 percent to the 40 to 50 percent range.

The banks, for their part, fought back with the introduction of free-interest rate CDs (in 1979) and so-called MMCs (money market certificates, in 1985), which had interest rates that followed those of CDs. The financial authorities accepted these movements in the private sector and agreed to exempt these new instruments from interest rate controls, and also promoted the liberalization of what hitherto had been controlled interest rates. Thus, in 1985, large-scale deposits of more than ¥1 billion saw interest rates liberalized, and thereafter the minimum deposit for such free rates was gradually lowered to ￥500 million, ￥300 million, ￥100 million, ￥50 million, and then ￥30 million in October 1988. Moreover, minimum denominations for CDs and MMCs were reduced along with the liberalization of their maturities, so that the only deposits that will be under strict interest rate controls of the old style by October 1989 are deposits of less than two weeks maturity and deposits of less than ￥3 million.

The process of financial liberalization in Japan had certain similarities to that in the United States, although the differences were also numerous. In the United States, there was an extremely short implementation period of three years after liberalization was adopted through the Depository Institutions Deregulation and Monetary Control Act of 1980, with full implementation by October 1983. In Japan's case, after the position taken in favor of liberalization in a Ministry of Finance report in May 1984, the process was implemented gradually. Second, as motivating forces for liberalization in the United States, there were not only the confrontations between banks and securities companies but also the demands of savings institutions; in Japan's case, pressure for liberalization from foreign financial institutions was strong. Third, interest rates on all small deposits in the United States were completely liberalized, while in Japan this liberalization is still in the transition period.

The biggest topic concerning liberalization in Japan will now be how to promote the liberalization of interest rates on all small deposits. The government has stated that in the interest of preparing the environment properly with regard to depositor protection and total balance of banks versus postal savings, discussion concerning the various detailed problems will take place in the near future and liberalization will be promoted after that of large deposits. As a proposal to implement this policy, an advisory body of the Ministry of Finance has suggested that "it would be realistic to begin the liberalization first by establishing small MMC accounts as a measure for the transition period." The problem, however, is whether complete liberalization of interest rates on small deposits could be implemented after the liberalization of small MMC interest rates. The reason for this is the existence of the postal savings system in Japan, a system that does not exist in the United States and that is much larger than similar systems in Europe.

Given the fact that the postal savings system holds one-third of all personal deposits, any move toward liberalizing interest rates on all small deposits, including postal savings deposits, would mean that the postal savings system, which is not based on the profit principle, would become the price leader in setting deposit interest rates and would exert strong influence over the interest rates offered by private financial institutions. There is a fear that such a course of events would result in interest rate formation entirely divorced from demand and supply conditions in the market. The problem is made more complicated by the fact that private financial institutions are under the supervision of the Ministry of Finance in all administrative matters, while the postal savings system is under the jurisdiction of the Ministry of Posts and Telecommunications, which would also make decisions on interest rate determination.

Relaxation of regulations on business activities
There are three major distinctions among types of financial business in Japan: the separation of banks from securities companies, the separation of banks from trust companies, and the separation of long-term from short-term finance. Such a clear distinction among types of business is, among the major industrial countries, unique to Japan. The reasons for these distinctions are as follows. First, because of the financial panics at the beginning of this century, there was

a recognition that it would be advantageous from the viewpoint of depositor protection and avoidance of conflict of interest for banks to specialize in short-term financial activities. Second, after the Second World War it was important to have institutions specializing in long-term finance, such as long-term credit banks and trust banks, in order to realize high rates of growth through exports and investment. Third, the separation of banking from the securities business was the result of policies during the occupation period in which the system in the United States was introduced somewhat abruptly; policy was formed with the notion of using specialized securities companies in order to develop securities markets that had previously been rather underdeveloped.

The comparisons with other industrial countries are striking. In the Federal Republic of Germany, there are no regulations separating various types of financial business since Germany has always been a country of universal banking. In France, long-term and short-term finance were separated from around 1940 until the middle of the 1960s, but since then there have been no controls of this sort or controls on trust or securities business. In the United Kingdom, there are no legal controls concerning the business of banks but there is a strong historical concept of commercial banking, so that in fact there has been a basic separation between long- and short-term finance and banking and securities businesses. Recently, however, this system has gradually been breaking down. In the United States, there are no financial institutions that specialize in long-term funds, but the tradition of commercial banking has been maintained so that the separation between banks and securities companies is closest to that of the situation in Japan. There are, however, some differences. In Japan, it is possible for banks to hold securities and stocks for investment purposes without corporate control, while such holdings are strictly prohibited in the United States. On the other hand, joint operation of trust business and banking business is relatively liberal in the United States but prohibited (with one exception) in Japan.

In recent years, the controls on business activities of financial institutions in Japan have been relaxed to a considerable extent. First, there has been a relaxation of the distinction between banks and securities companies. With the exception of the underwriting of securities, it was traditional in Japan to separate these businesses even in the prewar period. However, with the introduction of concepts from the U.S. Glass-Steagall Act of 1933 during the occupation period, the distinction between the two types of business was subject to absolute control, including the limiting of underwriting business to securities companies under Article 65 of the Securities Exchange Act. This same law excluded government bonds, local government bonds, and government guaranteed bonds from the underwriting prohibition, but, according to administrative guidance from the government, such underwriting was in fact prohibited for all but central government bonds. But conditions changed after the high-growth era. As banks faced the large-scale flotation of government bonds in the middle of the 1970s, they began to want to supply new financial instruments that included these government bonds, and therefore disputes sprang up between banks and the securities industry.

The disputes were settled in principle in 1981, with the new banking law and the revision of the Securities Exchange Act that clarified precisely which types of securities business banks could undertake. Under these laws banks were allowed to handle the subscription of funds for public bonds that they underwrote and were allowed to carry out business in the dealing of public bonds. On the other hand, the securities companies were allowed to create the so-called medium-term government bond fund, which is an investment trust similar to a deposit. Using this instrument, the securities companies have developed since 1984 a financial instrument that is almost identical to the cash management accounts (CMAs) of the United States. Even though the funds in such accounts travel through regular deposits, they have succeeded in giving the medium-term bond funds a definite settlement function. Moreover, the new laws approved loans by securities companies to customers on the collateral of government bonds. In addition, both banks and securities companies will be handling transactions in the bankers acceptance (BA) market and in the CP market that began in 1987. All of this means that the barriers between banks and securities companies have been falling and that a trend toward a further weakening of the distinctions in the future is occurring.

The distinction between long- and short-term financing is also weakening. Commercial banks are now increasing the proportion of medium- and long-term loans in their portfolios while the financial institutions that had specialized in long-term finance are increasing the short-term proportion of their portfolios. Thus, on the asset side, the maturity regulations are becoming meaningless. On the liability side, however, some distinctions remain: commercial banks are prohibited from taking deposits of more than two-year maturity while long-term credit banks are still allowed to raise funds of five-year maturity. Because of this situation, a mismatch of assets and liabilities has occurred, and in response the commercial banks have moved to circumvent these regulations by such mechanisms as interest rate swaps. It is therefore likely that barriers on the liability side will be reduced by allowing bond flotations and long-term CD issues by commercial banks in the Euromarket, along with the development of longer-term deposits in the domestic markets.

The distinction between banks and trust companies is

also becoming weaker. In earlier years, the main source of funding of trust banks was the pooling of long-term money trusts and loan trusts. Now, however, as the distinction between short- and long-term financing on the liability side is reduced, these trust funds are becoming indistinguishable from long-term time deposits. Moreover, in the pension trust business, which was the original area of business for trust companies, both domestic and foreign criticism against entry barriers is strengthening, precisely because this is such a growth area. It is inevitable that barriers of this type will be reduced.

Another barrier problem was pointed out in the Corrigan Report in the United States in January 1987: the barrier between commerce and finance. In Japan, however, this barrier is not such a pressing problem at the moment, for several reasons. The first is that holding companies are not permitted in Japan, which closes off the most convenient method for entering financial industries. Second, there is an incentive in the United States to begin nationwide financial service business in the form of nonbank banks in order to overcome regulations concerning interstate banking. In Japan, no such incentives exist. Third, equity in banks in Japan is relatively widely held, and stock owners see it as a long-term investment. In the future, however, these problems are almost certain to become important in Japan as well. When they do, the best approach would be, as pointed out in the Corrigan Report, to make distinctions among financial institutions according to their involvement in settlements business and then to list precisely which institutions may carry out settlements along with the other types of business that may be carried out by such institutions. The reason for this approach is that stability of the settlement system is the most important basis for the financial system as a whole.

There is a need to consider very cautiously whether it

is appropriate for Japan to adopt the method of entry into financial industries through the establishment of holding companies, especially with specific mention of this method in any of the proposals. In the prewar period, such holding companies existed, but they were used by financial conglomerates as a means of corporate control, and therefore were prohibited by the antimonopoly laws of the postwar period. Currently there are two schools of thought in Japan on whether to allow holding companies: one posits that they would speed the elimination of regulations; the other points to the possibility that they might promote concentration or monopoly.

The Corrigan Report also included a proposal for stabilizing the settlement system through the establishment of a federal electronic payments corporation. In Japan's case, there is a need to study any such proposal very carefully because of the influence that a third party might have in the provision of settlements services that are currently handled in a cooperative system between the central bank and private banks.

Regulations, customs, and orderly credit conditions
There are several elements in the financial safety net in Japan, both ex-ante and ex-post ones. The main ex-ante elements include primarily portfolio regulations such as capitalization ratio, liquidity ratio, and loan concentration ratio controls, along with supervision and inspection provisions, all of which are applied to financial institutions. The main ex-post elements of the safety net are the central bank's lender-of-last-resort function and the deposit insurance system. The framework for this safety net is largely the same as that in the United States and other advanced countries, with no notable differences.

Japan does, however, have certain unique features in this regard, and these lie in the actual administrative operation of the safety net along with the financial customs that support orderly credit conditions. Among these special features, the most important are the principle of collateral, the limits to entry and exit for banks, and the supervision system.

First, let us consider the principle of collateral in financial transactions. Both corporate bond flotations and interbank transactions in Japan are carried out under the principle of collateralization. In earlier years, bank lending was also collateralized, but in recent years there has been a major decline in the degree of collateralization of loans because of the large increase in foreign lending. Nevertheless, even today the degree of collateralization is 30 percent for city banks (60 percent if one includes guarantees), a rather high ratio. This principle, like others, was based on the experience of financial panics of earlier years and became a voluntary, settled practice on the part of private financial institutions.

With internationalization, this feature of the Japanese financial system has been reconsidered. In the long-term bond market, there has been a major relaxation of the issue conditions for noncollateralized bonds, and two bond-rating institutions were established in April 1985. In the short-term money market, noncollateralized call transactions were permitted in 1987 in response to the desires of foreign banks and other participants. The commercial paper market that began operation in the autumn of 1987 is also a noncollateralized market, so that hereafter the noncollateralized portion of transactions is expected to grow, centering on commercial paper and corporate bonds. In order, however, for such a situation to come about, it is urgent that the system of ratings be perfected.

Concerning restrictions on bank entry and exit, there are major differences in tradition and practice between the United States and Japan. In the United States, it is traditional for banks to enter and exit the industry, a tradition going back to the so-called free banking era from 1837 to 1863. In Japan, entry was allowed in the prewar period, but now there is a principle that new banks cannot be established and existing banks cannot be allowed to fail. These differences in tradition and principle have resulted in very different characteristics with regard to bankruptcies, in both the prewar and postwar periods. In the period of financial panics in the United States, the number of banks fell from 30,291 in 1920 to 14,361 in 1940, mostly due to failures. In Japan during this period, even though the number of banks fell from 2,063 in 1920 to 63 in 1940, most of the eliminated banks were saved by provision of liquidity from the central bank, merged with other banks, and thus were reabsorbed into the banking system. In the postwar period in the United States, entry and exit have remained common; in 1987, for example, more than 200 new banks were established, and 184 closed their doors. In Japan, there has not been a single new bank established since 1950, with the exception of certain special cases such as conversions of institutions from one form to another. Neither has there been a single bankruptcy of a Japanese bank, nor a single use of the deposit insurance system since its inception in 1971; there have been cases of problem banks, but these were taken care of by mergers. In the future, the liberalization of finance suggests that more emphasis will be placed on individual responsibility in the management of banks, and for this reason the deposit insurance system was expanded in 1986. One should not, of course, jump to the conclusion that bank failures will begin to occur in Japan because of such changes.

The third unique feature in Japan lies in certain differences in the supervisory system between Japan and other countries. The most important are as follows.

1) In Japan, the licensing for all types of financial institutions is concentrated in the Ministry of Finance, and

this applies not only to banks but to credit cooperatives, government-related financial institutions, securities companies, insurance companies, and the deposit insurance organization. The only exception is the postal savings system, which is under the supervisory authority of the Ministry of Posts and Telecommunications. In contrast, the approval and supervisory system in the United States is extremely complicated.

2) The Bank of Japan can transact business with all the various types of financial institutions in the domestic economy, and thus it has supervisory and regulatory powers concerning orderly credit conditions and financial policy for all of the clients with which it has concluded transactions contracts. For example, the Bank of Japan has opened transactions accounts and lending agreement contracts with securities companies. As a result, it can carry out supervision of the securities companies that is similar to that carried out vis-à-vis banks. In other major industrial countries, central banks do not in principle have such transactions with securities companies, so that other governmental organizations such as the Securities and Exchange Commission (SEC) in the United States carry out the supervisory and regulatory functions.

3) In supervisory and regulatory activities vis-à-vis financial institutions, stress is placed on the role of supervision and inspection.

The consequence of these provisions is that each financial institution in the country is inspected by the Bank of Japan and the Ministry of Finance every second year; that is to say, there is on-the-spot inspection for every financial institution every year. The reasons for this approach are that there are limits to the effectiveness of regulations such as those on capitalization and that it is difficult to check the soundness of management of an institution without assessing asset quality at the micro level. This approach does have disadvantages, including the extreme burden that it places on the authorities and the difficulty of understanding the outcome for depositors and investors. Because of such disadvantages, foreign countries in general place more emphasis on indicator regulations; in the United Kingdom and the Federal Republic of Germany, for example, on-the-spot supervision is not conducted at all. In addition to the type of regulation mentioned above, improvements such as the supervision of EDP activities are being made in order to adapt to new conditions.

Major Trends: Computerization and Globalization

In considering future issues of financial reform in Japan, two major trends must be considered: the transition from a settlements system based on information recorded on pieces of paper to one based on information recorded electronically, and the globalization of finance.

From paper money to electronic money
With the development of IC cards and electronic funds transfers, the settlements system is now undergoing a major change. The history of settlement systems is one of transition from such commodity currencies as rice, arrowheads, or gold dust to such metallic currencies as gold and silver coins, and thereafter to paper currency. The next transition, to electronic money, is an innovation of equal importance.

There are two common failures in periods of transition of the settlements system. One is fluctuation in the value of currency resulting from the confusion that arises in the process of monetary control, and the other is contagious credit crises that occur as payment defaults occur. In the interwar period, for example, there was a shift from the gold standard to a managed currency system, and from settlement in metallic currencies to settlement in paper currencies. At this time, Japan, along with the rest of the world, experienced the two types of crises mentioned above. As Japan moved from the Taishō era (1911–1926) into the Shōwa era (1926–1989), there were repeated financial crises, and the country experienced both deep deflation under Finance Minister Inoue and inflation under Finance Minister Takahashi. At the same time in the world at large there was the great depression of 1929.

The current transition from paper to electronic money, if not handled properly, poses the danger of repeating these two failures. The transition certainly represents progress from the point of view of efficiency, and must be pursued with a forward-looking attitude of innovation, as was the abolition of the gold standard. But sufficient care must be taken with respect to the preparation of laws and rules in order to avoid the difficulties of increased system risk and the danger of the loss of monetary control.

For example, in Japan there has been a rapid dissemination of private cards for use in transactions, like the telephone cards distributed by the telephone company (NTT) or the prepaid fare cards distributed by the recently privatized former national railroad (JR). These cards register funds paid for later debit against the services of these organizations. Information concerning the debits is processed in a memory built into the card itself. The issuers of such cards have so far been institutions with relatively high credit, and the cards have been limited to specific uses such as telephones and railroad fares. However, if any person or institution can issue such cards, and if their use becomes widespread, then there are implications for the monetary system. A considerable portion of Bank of Japan notes issued might be replaced by general-use cards. If that were to occur, two problems would come to the fore.

First, the ratio of base money (Bank of Japan notes plus Bank of Japan deposits) to the money supply—that is, the money multiplier—would rise along with this economization of Bank of Japan notes. The value of this multiplier would then become destabilized and difficult to predict, with the resulting possibility of confusion in control of the money supply. Second is the possibility of disorderly credit conditions in case of bankruptcy of a financial institution or corporation that had issued such cards. In such a case, firms that had sold goods against such payments could not claim recovery, and individuals could no longer use such cards and thus could not recover the funds remaining in the card memories. This would be the situation if suddenly bank notes became useless.

Because electronic cards are convenient and efficient, it is important to create appropriate policies in order to utilize the experience of the past on the basis of a forward-looking evaluation of their benefits. Various policies may be considered, including inspection of the creditworthiness of card-issuing institutions, management of secret ciphers that would be included in cards, and deposit of reserves at the Bank of Japan corresponding to funds paid into such cards in case of generalized use. It is important to avoid repeating the mistakes of the past that would turn the cogwheels of history backward.

There are two similar problems in the dissemination of electronic funds transfer (EFT) technology, which links computer and telecommunications technology. These are the problems of globalization and network building of settlement systems solely for electronic money. In any transaction, there are four separate stages: first, the gathering of market information; second, the conclusion of a transaction contract; third, the delivery of the commodities to be exchanged; and fourth, the settlement of funds, which includes in itself two substages, the transmission of settlement information and the delivery of means of payment. In the era of paper money the first was generally performed by newspapers and magazines, the second by contract documents, the third by actual goods transfers or book entries on custodial accounts, the first part of the fourth through bills, checks, or payments drafts, and the second part of the fourth through the delivery of bank notes or through book entries concerning deposit transfers.

Some of these stages of certain transactions have already come under electronic systems, as part of the globalization of finance. For example, the first stage can be conducted in an electronic form through the Reuters monitor (for foreign exchange transactions) and the Telerate and Quick systems (for interest rate transactions). The second stage is electronically available under the Reuters dealing system (for foreign exchange). The third stage is provided electronically under the Euro-Clear system and the CEDEL system for Eurobonds and under the DTC system (for corporate bonds in the United States). The fourth stage is provided under the Fed wire system, in which settlement of funds is simultaneous with delivery of services.

Once all of these various stages of transactions are united in a single network, it will be useless to talk about payments facilities as a sacred area of bank business. The first three stages and the first substage of the fourth can easily be carried out by nonfinancial institutions such as value-added-network (VAN) operators. The second part of the fourth stage might also be carried out by VAN operators if settlements were offset against each other on a one-for-one basis. New payments balances that could not be offset in this fashion would have to be settled through the accounts of financial institutions but not necessarily through bank deposits. If, for example, investment trusts or insurance premiums were financial assets that could be created and canceled instantaneously, they could be used to transfer means of settlement through real time processing, even if the principle in such accounts were not of a certain value. If this were to occur, bank deposits would be used only by customers who refused to accept investment trusts or insurance premiums.

Within such networks, unpaid settlement balances would be transferred from the nonfinancial sector to the financial sector or from the nonbank sector to the bank sector, but even the banking sector itself would not finalize the payment through the transfer of deposits among customers. There would remain lending and borrowing relationships between the banks of the two parties that were transferring the deposits. Final payment would only become possible with transfer of central bank notes or deposits between the two institutions. In other words, the only institution that can supply complete finality to a transaction is the central bank. There is always an accumulated unpaid balance for other payment methods that are provided by private institutions.

There are other problems as well. First, if networks are constructed that go all the way from individual corporations to the central bank, there is the fear of direct access to liquidity and therefore confusion in financial adjustments. There is also a system risk—that is, the danger of contagious insolvencies that could occur if one actor in a network of participating firms or institutions suspended payment, with the result of accumulating unpaid balances in the network as a whole.

Thus, it is clear that there are many difficult problems associated with EFT and the financial system; still, it would be foolish to try to stop the development of such systems on those grounds. As computer and telecommunications costs fall, the layer structure of such networks will become more simplified, and therefore the efficiency of settlements and thus the efficiency of the economy as a whole will increase. Such systems must be evaluated from the point of view of future appropriateness.

Moreover, if the development of such systems in Japan were to fall behind, then, as pointed out in the discussion of the globalization of finance, the settlements system in Japan would be absorbed into the settlement networks centering on the United States and Europe. For example, even now it is possible to connect branches of banks in New York and Tokyo through on-line systems, so that safe and convenient U.S. dollar settlements may be achieved through connections of terminals over the Fed wire in New York. Moreover, links between Tokyo and the SWIFT system allow ECU settlement through payment instructions to the Bank for International Settlements in Basel, Switzerland. Even the delivery of securities can be handled in this way. For example, through the link between the Mark-III system of the GE Corporation and SWIFT, instructions can be given to Euro-Clear and the CEDEL system allowing delivery of Eurobonds and Euro-CDs. If 24-hour operations become possible in the future, the risk involved will decline substantially.

In order for Japan to become the third great financial center of the world, along with New York and London, it is necessary to construct a convenient, safe yen settlement system and securities delivery network in Tokyo and to plan for the globalization of this system. In order to do this there are two problems that must be tackled. One of these will be dealt with in detail in the next section of this chapter: the relaxation of regulations that are preventing the development of such a system and the standardization across countries of systems and practices.

But first we must discuss the necessity for a yen clearing system and the risk policy for it. There will be increased need for transparent rules for those participating in the settlement network and for supervision and examination of the participants. It will also be necessary to develop mechanisms to reduce the system risk of operations and to reduce the accumulation of unpaid balances within such a system. It might be appropriate to discuss the introduction of obligation netting, which would prevent the accumulation of such balances by offsetting liabilities and assets at the time they occur even though the settlement date for such assets and liabilities might not yet have arrived.

The essence of a risk-avoidance policy is the reduction to the greatest extent possible of the time that elapses within the network for stages two to four of any transaction. The ultimate form of such a system is the creation of the "Nichigin Net," with continuous final settlement. In such a system, terminals are distributed in private-sector banks, and if customers so wish, the system will complete payments in real time through transfer of Bank of Japan balances. If such a system develops, then there will be a gradual simplification of the four-tier network that includes the nonfinancial sector, the nonbank financial sector, the banking sector, and the central bank. Through such a system the accumulation of unpaid balances would be avoided, and a safe and efficient expansion of trade and payments could occur. The United States is already moving in this direction with the Fed wire. In order to maintain the ability of the central bank to influence financial conditions and to maintain appropriately its function as lender of last resort, such a yen clearing system is desirable. The Nichigin Net actually started operation in the autumn of 1988.

The globalization of finance

It has been many years since the term "internationalization of finance" has come into general use. This term means that the financial systems of various countries have developed relationships that extend across national borders. As a result, the financial systems in those countries have been subject to international influence, and that influence has triggered financial innovation, liberalization, and reform.

The term "financial globalization" takes this concept one step further in nuance. Instead of the financial systems of various countries being related across borders and influencing one another, the wider term "globalization" indicates a further strengthening of the ties among these markets so that they have actually changed into a unified financial system on a worldwide scale. Of course "worldwide scale" indicates only the unification of the markets of the industrial countries and includes neither the markets of developing countries nor those of the Eastern bloc. Moreover, the core of this unified financial system is composed of the financial and capital markets of New York, Tokyo, and London. Still, through electronic networks connecting these three markets, it has become possible to carry out business around the clock; thus the phrase "worldwide scale" is in fact justified. No matter which longitude or latitude the developing or Eastern bloc countries are situated in, they also have the opportunity to participate chronologically in this network.

Several aspects of this financial globalization are in fact proceeding. The first aspect of financial globalization is the "globalization of financial markets," in the sense that financial transactions may be carried out in the currency of choice by freely entering or exiting the financial markets of different countries. Both the financial institutions and corporations use a wide variety of transactions as they seek to maximize profits. These institutions and corporations participate in all types of transactions worldwide, observe developments around the clock, respond as necessary, and conduct business in the market that is open at the particular time they seek to execute transactions.

In addition, recent years have seen financial institutions using telecommunications across international borders to conduct business directly from their home offices. As a result, markets in different parts of the world have in fact been unified functionally as a single market, thus giving rise to the term "the global marketplace."

In order to participate in global transactions, it is necessary to have methods of transaction that allow access to foreign markets. The development and provision of such methods of transaction are now progressing under the term "global business" or "globalized services." The first requirement for globalized transactions is the establishment of monitoring systems to keep track of the information necessary to carry out these transactions. The second requirement is a dealing system that allows the transactions to take place. Apart from information gathering in a relatively narrow scope and carrying out standardized transactions, the full-fledged operation of businesses requires a business presence in the markets in question. This is the third requirement for globalized transactions. Financial institutions in particular have built business operations worldwide. For example, there were only 81 foreign banks in New York in 1970, but this figure had grown to 253 by the end of 1980 and to 435 by the end of June 1987.

In addition to the globalization of the methods of transactions, it is also necessary for there to be globalization of the settlement mechanism. Through this globalization of settlements, there will be a feedback effect that will provide additional stimulus to the markets involved. This globalized settlement system need not be limited merely to the settlement of funds but could very well be extended to the delivery and settlement of numerous financial market products and securities. For the delivery systems of financial instruments and securities to be useful, the instruments must take a form that is convenient for delivery. In this sense, the so-called securitization of financial transactions and the globalization of settlement systems are very closely interrelated.

Globalization is likely to increase the need for transactions that involve multiple currencies. Globalization will thus promote the development of techniques for redenomination of currency contracts, and this in turn will stimulate globalization. This feedback loop will exist because the facilitation of redenomination will allow financial institutions and corporations to utilize foreign currency-denominated instruments while avoiding foreign exchange risk. One traditional method of redenomination is the forward exchange contract. In recent years, the choice of such financial instruments has broadened dramatically. Examples include futures, currency swaps, and options. For futures and options trading, there is a strong need for investors to be able to adjust their positions on a 24-hour basis. This need has become an opportunity for the exchanges in various countries to cooperate in the formation of mutual settlement mechanisms. That is, these futures and options, which originally were developed as a means of redenomination, have now come to be traded in their own right.

Reasons for financial globalization
The above paragraphs outlined the current state of financial globalization. We must now ask why globalization has proceeded so steadily. There are three basic reasons for its steady progress. The first is that the precursors of globalization, financial reform and liberalization, proceeded in a similar form in all of the major countries. As a result of this process, a common foundation has made financial globalization easier. The reason why financial reform proceeded in parallel in most G-7 countries after the shift to floating exchange rates is that all faced new technological and economic conditions that exaggerated the frictions within the old financial system. The four most important of those new conditions can be summarized as follows.

First, as macroeconomic performance became less stable after the shift to floating exchange rates, interest rates became subject to sharp changes and wild gyrations. These movements created intense friction with the interest rate regulations of the old financial system. Second, there was an important revolution in computer information and telecommunications technology that had a major impact on the financial sector. Through these advances, financial institutions were able to produce many new financial instruments and to reduce substantially the costs of supplying financial services to their clients. These events created pressure to eliminate the regulations that separated financial business into different segments. Third, after the shift to floating exchange rates, there was a major increase in international capital flows. This development generated severe friction with the principle of separation of foreign and domestic capital markets, which was embodied in the exchange controls of the old system. The fourth condition was the expansion of fiscal deficits in the major countries. These deficits generated large increases in the amounts of government bonds issued, and therefore not only fostered the development of open markets, but also encouraged the "securitization of finance" and caused friction with the interest rate regulations and the business separation regulations under the old system.

In this way, the four new conditions came into conflict with the interest rate regulations, business activity regulations, and the exchange controls that had comprised the framework of the old financial system. These four conditions also became the driving force behind the simultaneous adoption in several countries of financial reforms that eventually liberalized interest rates and rewrote business activity regulations.

The second reason for the globalization of finance is the increased volume of international capital flows in recent years. This is due to two factors: 1) the shift to a floating exchange rate system and 2) reduced opportunities for real investment in certain economies. The latter is attributable to the reduction in real growth rates of the countries involved, which occurred simultaneously with the change in exchange rate systems. The third reason is the development of tele-communications and computer technologies facilitating the increased international flow of capital.

Globalization and the need for international regulatory standards

The relaxation of regulations has been an important factor in making possible the globalization of finance. However, the advance of globalization itself has also had the effect of increasing the pressure for an international standardiza-tion of regulations.

A major issue has been the competition among financial systems accompanying the intensification of competition among markets. In a globalized world, financial institutions and corporations may freely use the markets and systems of their choice; therefore, when the financial system regula-tions of one country are more burdensome or costly for private business than those of another country, market participants will flee to the country with the least demanding regulations. This process is known as the "hollowing-out of the financial sector." As a result of this, some countries carry out reforms of their regulatory structures with the hope that business will accrue to their financial institutions and markets. This factor was important in the establishment of offshore markets in several countries and in the Big Bang in the City of London.

In Japan, however, changes in regulations have not fol-lowed this pattern, but have in fact run contrary to it. Japa-nese financial reform has so far been implemented only after reform had taken place in markets overseas. This meant that the Japanese market became relatively less attractive to investors, precisely the reverse outcome of the "com-petition among systems" strategy mentioned above. In this sense, one might say that there was an artificial hollowing-out of the Japanese markets. As a result, fund-raising and investment by Japanese corporations shifted abroad, and at the same time the Japanese financial institutions handling these transactions saw their market shares in foreign markets grow to a level that was called "over-presence" and that brought adverse reactions. It is indeed unfortunate that these factors led to an unnecessary increase in international economic friction. Now that Japanese financial authorities have reassessed the situation, deregulation in the domestic market will occur in line with that abroad, and the international standardization of regulations will proceed, even in the Japanese market.

Another problem concerning the regulatory aspect of globalization is the so-called level playing field issue that has become prominent with the growing competition among market participants. In contrast to the strategy of competition among systems in which countries seek to make their own markets and systems more attractive, the level playing field approach attempts to change regulations in other countries so that one's own financial institutions are not at a disadvantage.

Concerning the entry and activities of foreign financial institutions, the major industrial countries have for many years adopted a policy of "national treatment in principle" for foreign institutions, meaning "equal treatment between counterpart-country and home-country citizens without discrimination." But even if country A and country B both applied the principle of national treatment, it would not necessarily mean that foreign financial institutions in country A would be treated the same as foreign financial institutions in country B. According to the principle of national treatment, such differences were permitted. With the globalization of financial markets and the intensification of competition among financial institutions of the major countries, however, several developments occurred. The first was that those countries where financial deregulation was proceeding at a relatively rapid pace pressured countries where deregulation was progressing more slowly to fulfill their promises of national treatment.

A second development was the introduction of the concept of "reciprocity." The new banking law of Japan in 1981 used this reciprocity concept, and in the United Kingdom's Financial Services Act of 1986, Part 9 introduced a section on reciprocity.

The third development was extraterritorial application of domestic national regulations. This issue has become conspicuous in cases where it is thought that the aims of domestic regulations may not or cannot be realized unless applied externally. Extraterritoriality became a public issue in 1979 when the United States extended its freeze on Iranian assets to the dollar deposits of foreign branches of U.S. banks. This was, however, already a general problem in the structure of U.S. laws. Extraterritoriality is an aggressive method of addressing these problems in that it unilaterally forces on other countries solutions to problems that involve the sovereignty of several countries. Moreover, its effects extend beyond the activities in foreign markets of financial institutions of the home country and those who wish to enter domestic markets. With the progress of globalization, "level playing field" problems emerge because of this globalization. In the end, these issues develop into problems of international cooperation among the public authorities of different countries or problems of standardization of regulations among countries through multifaceted discussions. For example, the United States and the United Kingdom had agreed on common standards for bank capitalization and asked Japan and other countries in 1987 to adjust their practices according to those standards. An accord on common "capital adequacy" regulation was reached at the Bank for International Settlements. In the past, capital adequacy regulations were methods for individual countries to strengthen and support the ability of banks to face risks. However, in a globalized financial world, differences in regulations between countries have affected the relative competitive situations faced by the financial institutions of different countries, and this has led to a groundswell of support for equalizing competitive conditions through the establishment of common standards.

An important background factor in the demands for equalization of standards was the rapid growth in the international influence of Japanese banks. The broad historical trend of globalization will force major decisions on financial regulation in Japan. As the twenty-first century approaches, it will be necessary to create a new world financial system that acknowledges two historical realities, the globalization of finance and the change of the major creditor nation from the United States to Japan. Within this new financial system, the Japanese yen and the Tokyo financial and capital markets will play a major role and thus lighten the excessive burden that has been shouldered so far by the U.S. dollar and the New York markets. As suggested in Chapter IV, a trilateral currency system based on the U.S. dollar, the yen, and the Deutsche-mark or the ECU under the floating exchange rate system combined with closer policy coordination, including fiscal policy, is the most likely scenario for the future. The essential basis for such a currency system is no doubt the globalized financial system centered on the New York, Tokyo, and London markets.

Problems for the Future

This chapter has shown that financial innovation in Japan has proceeded to a considerable extent, and that further progress is expected under the influence of technological advances such as electronic money and the need for financial globalization. The issue remains, however, of how to make the financial system as safe as possible.

There are many meanings to the phrase "the safety of the financial system," but in Japan two are of particular importance. The first is whether a new financial system built to conform with the facts of the Japanese economy will also conform with conditions in the rest of the world. As discussed above, there is a need to plan for the internationalization of regulations, so that new financial systems can simultaneously be safe and satisfy the financial needs of a continuously globalizing world. This point is especially important for Japan, which not only accounts for one-tenth of the world economy but also has now become the world's largest creditor nation. The second important aspect of safety concerns the issue of whether the various functions that are expected of a financial system (intermediation, risk diversification, and settlement) can be carried out as safely in the new system as in the old. The difficulties are amplified by the technological progress of the movement toward an electronic payment system. As touched upon earlier, and as pointed out in the Corrigan Report, the most important requirement is that the safety of the settlement system not be harmed, since the settlement system is the very basis for society and the economy. This function is the most basic role carried out by a financial system. Let us therefore once again consider two more aspects of these issues, the internationalization of regulations and securing the safety of the payment mechanism.

Harmonization of international regulations

The globalization of finance became possible in part because of the relaxation of regulations, but globalization itself has brought pressure to change regulations, in the feedback loop already mentioned. If domestic stability is given too much weight and defended to excess, then ironically there will be insufficient international harmonization and in the end the system itself will destabilize. An example of this is the issue of how to respond to the competition among systems that is the result of jockeying for position among international markets. Every country, to a certain extent, has been carrying out changes in regulations with a view to attracting the business of home markets and institutions.

Although it is necessary to carry out financial reform from an international point of view, there are many substantive points to consider. One of these is whether the competition among systems of the major countries might have a tendency to become excessive. Precisely because banking in the offshore markets is more difficult to regulate and to supervise than in domestic markets, there is a need for caution to avert excessive competition. For this reason, the Bank of Japan has for a long time promoted complementarity between the growth of offshore markets and the liberalization of domestic markets.

Another problem that faces regulators in an era of globalization is that of regulations to level the playing field, which accompany more fierce competition among agents and the market. As discussed above, this approach contrasts with the competition among systems, which attempts to improve the attractiveness of the home-country system, and instead attempts to change the regulations in foreign countries with the intention of correcting the disadvantages of home-country markets or financial institutions. The United States and the United Kingdom established joint standards for bank capitalization at the beginning of 1987, and called for harmonization with these regulations by other countries, including Japan. Japan's response was that Japanese financial customs avoided reduction of capital at times of crisis and rebuilt losses through the sales of stocks held below market value in the portfolio. Therefore, if a portion of the unrealized gains on these stocks could be included in the definition of capital, Japan would agree to the new system. In fact, capitalization ratios in Japan include 70 percent of these unrealized gains in the definition of capital; using these amounts, the capitalization ratios for city banks in fact come to 8 to 10 percent. When such unrealized gains are excluded, the capitalization ratios fall below 3 percent.

One outcome of intense discussion among several nations was a report entitled "International Convergence of Capital Measurement and Capital Standards" issued in July 1987 by the Committee on Banking Regulations and Supervisory Practices of the Bank for International Settlements. The report establishes uniform capital ratios which all the major banks in the G-10 countries and Luxembourg must achieve by the end of 1992. According to this plan, 45 percent of the difference between the book value and the market value of equity holdings is counted as part of capital; this represents a concession to Japan's proposal.

This problem is related to other differences among the systems of countries, such as the collateral principle and regulations on types of business which banks may engage in, which were discussed in an earlier section. Banks in Japan usually require collateral or security of some sort when making loans, and in the postwar period there has been no bank bankruptcy. Another such difference is that the United States, under the Glass-Steagall Act of 1933, forbids equity investment by banks; the Securities Exchange Law in Japan, under Article 65, does not forbid such holdings. Of course, it is not true that American banks have nothing to do with stock holdings since, in fact, equities are held as investments in the trust accounts of these banks. In Japan the joint operation of banking activities and trust activities in a single institution is not permitted. In the process of standardization of regulations, it will be necessary to strengthen the mutuality of the financial systems in different countries and for systems to converge on a middle ground.

Stability of the payment system

As a part of the process of financial reform, the payment system is changing greatly. One of the problems, as discussed above, is the increase in system risk, which will be defined here as follows: a paralysis of function of the payment system caused by a process of sequential inability to pay on the part of financial institutions as a result of the inability of one institution that participates in the system to meet its payments to other institutions which had expected to pay yet others on the basis of the receipt of these funds. That is, system risk is a danger of collapse of credit conditions because of an external diseconomy.

Some points could be added to the discussion. With the liberalization of finance, there is an increase in interest rate risk, liquidity risk, credit risk, and exchange risk; as a result, there is increased possibility of collapse of management on the part of participants in the payment system. There has also been an enormous increase in amounts settled that has accompanied the increase in international payments and the development of electronic funds transfer; as a result, there has been increased possibility of accidents. There is an even more fundamental problem: the loss of so-called finality in the payment of debts through the delivery of bank notes, because payment is increasingly made through checks, credit cards, and automatic transfers provided by private financial institutions and not through bank notes supplied by a central bank; as a result, there has been an increase in the outstanding balance of unpaid bills. Just as for the exchange of bills and domestic exchange in the private settlement system, a payment is not in fact completed when the creditor receives funds, because an interbank settlement is still required to complete the transaction.

Interbank settlements, however, are not made on a case-by-case basis but rather are settled multilaterally among participating banks, with all of the settlements on a particular day made as a group. The reason for the increase in importance of facilities for concentrated settlement in the private sector in place of the finality of bank notes is that such facilities are more efficient. This is what makes system risk such an important problem. There are several methods that are available in order to avoid system risk. For example, in the United States there is a so-called cap policy that places an upper limit on unpaid balances. This policy, however, faces constraints in its practical application. A more fundamental solution would be the reduction of unpaid balances through the recovery of finality. As technological progress reduces the cost of final case-by-case settlements, there will no longer be the need to raise dependence on concentrated settlements in the private sector to the point of ignoring heightened risk. In the United States, not only government securities but other types of transactions as well are now being settled either on the Fed wire or through individual settlement using deposits at the Federal Reserve. All of these types of settlement have finality and therefore may be thought of as services that are equivalent to "electronic bank notes."

In Japan, too, there is a clear social need for such convenient electronic bank notes and for an appropriate response through cooperation between the Bank of Japan and private financial institutions. Japan, however, does not have a securities settlement system like the Fed wire system for government securities in which the settlement of funds occurs at the same time as the delivery of securities, "delivery against payment." From the viewpoint of reducing risk, the introduction of such a system is becoming more important.

In addition to reducing the risk latent in the settlement system, it is important to adjust the safety net of traditional policies. Otherwise, the progress of financial reform will increase the burden on the existing safety net. If this occurs, there finally will be fear of an increased burden on bank management through the accumulation of payments reserves, increases in capitalization, and increases in deposit insurance premiums.

In this traditional safety net, it goes without saying that the first ex-ante element is the necessity for sound management based on the principle of self-responsibility. At the same time, there will be increased need for supervision and examination by public authorities. In the worst cases, there will also be the need for ex-post means to support orderly credit conditions centering on the lender-of-last-resort function of the central bank along with the deposit insurance system. An excess dependence, however, on these ex-post mechanisms would increase the so-called moral hazards, and it is necessary to remember that such a development might weaken the soundness of management. In order to maintain orderly credit conditions, proper use of the ex-ante mechanisms is essential for proper use of the ex-post mechanisms. In this sense, the two types of mechanisms can be complementary elements in planning for orderly, stable credit conditions.

Index

agricultural trade, 86, 97, 101–2, 109
Asia: export activities of, 79, 133–34; Japanese trade with, 132–35

Bank of Japan: control of money supply, 14–15, 18–22; definition of money stock, 5, 14; monetary policy of, 14–25; regulatory powers of, 150
banking crises, 95, 101, 102
banking systems, comparison of U.S. and Japanese, 148–51
Bretton Woods system, 29, 33, 113
business cycles, 71, 99, 110

capitalization, international standards for, 168–69
cash management accounts

(CMAs), 145
CEDEL system, 154, 156
central banks: role in electronic settlements systems of, 155–56; role as lender-of-last-resort of, 105
certificates of deposit (CDs), 140, 145
collateral, in Japanese financial transactions, 148, 168
commodity prices, 61, 82
Corrigan Report, 146, 147, 166
credit crises, 102, 105, 109, 151
creditor nations, major, 95–96, 101–2, 104–6, 111–13, 115–16, 117–18
current account balances, 32, 33, 35–36, 123–24, 125, 128–30
current account surpluses, recycling of, 97, 109, 110

173

debt crises, 56, 101–2
debtor nations, 94–95, 97, 102, 109, 113–15
deposit insurance system (Japan), 172
deposit rates, liberalization of Japanese, 20–22, 140–42
Deutsche-mark, 45, 56, 57, 94, 165
discount rates, 58, 60, 61, 83
dollar: clearing system for transactions in, 154; depreciation of, 39–40, 46–56; exchange value of, 39–40, 46–56, 66, 84; forward markets in, 45–46; as key currency in international monetary system, 38, 44, 96, 105, 107–9, 113–15; oversupply of, 33–34; overvaluation of, 107
domestic demand: in Europe, 61–62; in Japan, 63, 64, 69, 74–77, 79, 82; in the United States, 59–60

eclectic gradualism, 17
economic activity, VAR models of Japanese, 22–24
electronic bank notes, 171–72
electronic funds transfers (EFT), 152, 153–58, 169–70
electronic prepaid services cards, 152–53
Euro-Clear system, 154, 156
European Currency Unit (ECU), 117, 118, 132, 156, 165
European Monetary System (EMS), 119, 120
exchange rates: anchor rates for setting, 126–27; fixed, 6, 33–34; floating, 24–25, 29 –38, 78–79, 107, 120–24, 125; policy coordination

for management of, 55, 57–62, 106–7, 116–17, 125–27, 129–30
export restraints, 36
extraterritoriality, of financial regulations, 164, 167

Fed wire clearance system, 154, 156, 157, 171
financial institutions, regulation of Japanese, 142–51
financial regulations, globalization of, 164, 167
fixed exchange rate system, 6, 33–34
floating exchange rate system, 24–25, 29–38, 78–79, 107, 120–24, 125
France: economic performance of, 32, 34–35, 36, 37; financial business in, 143
front loading, of Japanese public expenditures, 74, 75, 78
Fukao, Mitsuhiro, 46

Germany: as creditor nation, 112–13; economic performance of, 32, 34–35, 36, 37; financial business in, 143; interest rates in, 61–62
Glass-Steagall Act, 144, 169
globalization, 157–60, 162–65, 166–67
gold standard, 95, 96, 98–99, 102–3, 107, 111, 113, 151
government bonds, Japanese, 137–38, 140
Gramm-Rudmann-Hollings Amendment, 41–42, 114–15
gorwth, stabilization of Japanese, 5–10, 13–14, 16–17, 24–25, 32, 62–63
growth rates, in G-5 countries,

compared, 30–32, 36–38

holding companies, 146, 147

industrial restructuring, in
    Japan, 69–70
inflation, in Japan, 7–10, 16–
    17, 82–83
interbank market rates, in Japan,
    18–20
interbank settlements, 171
interest rate differentials, 42,
    46–48, 49–52, 58–59,
    100, 129
interest rates: in the Federal
    Republic of Germany, 61–
    62; in Japan, 22, 25, 75,
    138, 139–41; in the United
    States, 40, 58–61
"International Convergence of
    Capital Measurement, and
    Capital Standards," 169
international monetary system,
    changes in key-currency
    nations in, 95–97, 104–5,
    111–13, 116
inventory adjustments, as
    response to the high yen,
    63–64, 67
investment adjustment, in Japan,
    64, 68, 76–77

Japan: banking system, 148–51,
    169–70, 171–72; current
    account surplus of, 53, 80–
    81, 118; domestic demand
    in, 63, 64, 69, 74–77, 79,
    81; economic performance
    of, 5–10, 13–14, 16–17,
    24–25, 32, 34–35, 81–84;
    financial business in, 142–
    46; financial liberalization
    in, 139–42; fiscal policy of,
    74, 81–83; government
    bond issues in, 137–38,

140; industrial restructuring
    in, 69–70; inflation rates in,
    7–10, 16–17, 82–84;
    interest rates in, 22, 25, 73,
    138, 139–41; investment
    adjustments in, 64, 68, 76–
    77; labor market in, 10–11;
    land use policies for, 71–
    72, 85; as largest creditor
    nation, 109, 116, 117–18;
    monetary policy of, 7, 14–
    17, 70–72, 75, 83–84;
    money function in, 26–29;
    money stock in, 5, 7, 18–
    22, 28–29, 80; regulation
    of financial institutions in,
    142–51; securities industry
    in, 142, 143; standard of
    living in, 84–85; tax reform
    for, 71, 86–88; trade
    balance of, 63, 64, 68, 78;
    trade with Asia, 80, 81, 79,
    132–35

key currencies: dollar, 38, 44,
    96, 105, 107–9, 113–15;
    multilateral system of,
    116–17, 118–20, 125–27,
    130–32, 155; pound, 95–
    97, 111–12; yen, 110,
    117–19, 135
Keynes Plan, 113
Keynesian theory, 10–11, 13

labor market, Japanese, 10–11
land use policy, for Japan, 71–
    72, 85
Latin America, 97, 102
London, 156, 158, 162
Louvre Accord, 55–56, 59,
    106–7

Maekawa Report, 130
Ministry of Finance (Japan),
    149–50

monetary policy, Japanese, 7,
14–17, 70–72, 75, 83–84
money, Bank of Japan definition
of, 5, 14
money function, in Japan, 26–
29
money games, 97, 99–100,
109–10
money market certificates
(MMCs), 140–41, 142
money stock: growth of, in
Japan, 5–7, 28–29, 80;
transmission channels for
change in Japanese, 18–22
money supply, control of by
central banks, 14–15, 105
multilateral currency system,
116–17, 118–20, 125–27,
130–32, 165

New York, 44, 95, 113, 119,
158, 159, 165
Newly Industrializing Economies, 80, 116, 133, 134
Nichigin Net, 157

offshore markets, 167
oil crises, 7, 25, 33, 34, 121

Pax Americana, 113
Pax Brittanica, 111
Pax Japonica, 116
Plaza Accord, 7, 39, 41, 42–43,
55, 58, 68
policy coordination, for management of exchange rates,
55, 57–62, 106–7, 116–
17, 125–27, 129–30
Postal Savings Bank (Japan),
140, 142, 150
pound: as key currency in international monetary system,
95–97, 111–12; overvalua-
tion of, 96, 99, 102, 107
price stability, 16–17, 124, 128

protectionism, 36, 43, 101–2,
115, 118, 124
purchasing power parity (PPP)
rates, 48–49, 84–85, 96,
122–23, 124, 125, 127–28

Quick system, 154

redenomination, 131, 160
Regulation Q (U.S.A.), 139
regulations, for financial
business activities, 161,
162–70
Reuters dealing system, 154
risk premium, of dollar holdings,
41, 44–46, 48

Securities Exchange Act (Japan),
144, 169
securities industry, in Japan,
142, 143
settlements system, 146–47,
151–52, 153–60, 166, 170
Smoot-Hawley tariffs, 101
Special Drawing Rights (SDRs),
132
standardization, of financial
regulations, 167–68
stock market crash: of October
1929, 95–98, 100–102,
104; of October 1987, 59,
108, 115
SWIFT system, 156

tax reform, for Japan, 71, 86–
88
Telerate system, 154
Tokyo, 118–19, 156, 158, 165
trade balances: Japan, 63, 64,
68, 78; United States, 52–
53, 113–14
transactions, under electronic
systems, 153–55, 158–59

unemployment, in the United

States, 59, 60–61
United Kingdom: economic
    performance of, 32, 34–35,
    37; economic performance
    of, in 1920s, 99; financial
    business in, 143; and the
    gold standard, 95, 96,
    98–99, 102, 107; as largest
    creditor nation, 95–97,
    104, 111
United States: budget deficit of,
    79, 107, 113–15; current
    account deficit of, 52–53,
    121; as debtor nation, 41,
    43, 107, 113–15; domestic
    demand in, 59–60;
    economic performance of,
    32, 34–35, 37–38, 42–44,
    58–61; economic policy
    during the Great Depres-
    sion, 98–103, 105–6;
    economic policy of Reagan
    administration, 40–42, 46,
    55, 57; financial business
    in, 143; financial liberaliza-
    tion in, 141; and the gold
    standard, 102–3; interest
    rates in, 40, 58–61; as

largest creditor nation,
    101–2, 104–5; role in the
    international economic
    system, 93–95, 104–6,
    113–15; trade balance of,
    52–53, 113–14; trade
    structure of, 134–35;
    unemployment in, 59,
    60–61

Venice Summit, 106–7

wage contracts, in Japan, 10–11
wealth effect, 70–71, 75
White Plan, 113
World War I, 98, 113
World War II, 106, 113

yen: appreciation of, 7, 25, 39–
    40, 46–49, 54–55, 63–64,
    66–70, 74, 81; clearing
    system for transactions in,
    156–57; exchange value
    of, 39–40, 46–56, 66, 84;
    as key currency in inter-
    national monetary system,
    110, 117–19, 135